OFFICE-HOLDERS IN MODERN BRITAIN

VIII
Foreign Office Officials
1782–1870

OFFICE-HOLDERS
IN MODERN BRITAIN

Volumes I–VI compiled by J. C. Sainty;
volume VII compiled by J. M. Collinge

I
Treasury Officials
1660–1870 (1972)

II
Officials of the Secretaries
of State
1660–1782 (1973)

III
Officials of the Boards
of Trade
1660–1870 (1974)

IV
Admiralty Officials
1660–1870 (1975)

V
Home Office Officials
1782–1870 (1975)

VI
Colonial Office Officials
1794–1870 (1976)

VII
Navy Board Officials
1660–1832 (1978)

The above volumes, the first five of which were formerly published by the Athlone Press, are now published and distributed by the University of London, Institute of Historical Research, Senate House, Malet Street, London WC1E 7HU

OFFICE-HOLDERS
IN MODERN BRITAIN

VIII

Foreign Office Officials 1782–1870

compiled by
J. M. COLLINGE

UNIVERSITY OF LONDON
INSTITUTE OF HISTORICAL RESEARCH
1979

Published and distributed by
UNIVERSITY OF LONDON
INSTITUTE OF HISTORICAL RESEARCH
Senate House
Malet Street
London WC1E 7HU

0 901179 55 8

Printed in Great Britain by
WESTERN PRINTING SERVICES LTD
BRISTOL

Contents

Abbreviations

app. appointed, appointment
Bart. Baronet
c. circa
cr. created
d. death, died
Dept. Department
dis. dismissed
ed. edited, edition
f., ff. folio, folios
HC House of Commons Paper
Hon. Honourable
occ. occurrence, occurs
pd. paid
pt. part
reapp. reappointed
Rept. Report
res. resigned
ret. retired
succ. succeeded
TM Treasury Minute

References

IN MANUSCRIPT

British Library, London

Add. MS 28063; Egerton MS 3505	Leeds Papers.
Add. MS 58968, 59229	Dropmore Papers.

Public Record Office, London

C 66	Patent Rolls.
FO 83	Foreign Office: Great Britain and General.
FO 84	Foreign Office: Slave Trade Correspondence.
FO 96	Foreign Office: Miscellanea, Series II.
FO 366	Foreign Office: Chief Clerk's Department Archives.
HO 38	Home Office: Warrant Books.
PC 2	Privy Council Registers.
Prob. 11	Prerogative Court of Canterbury: Registered Copies of Wills.
T 52	Treasury: King's Warrants.
T 53	Treasury: Warrants Relating to Money.

WORKS IN PRINT

Dip. Rep.	*British Diplomatic Representatives 1789–1852*, ed. S. T. Bindoff, E. F. Malcolm Smith and C. K. Webster. Camden 3rd ser., l, 1934.
1st Rept. on Fees	*First Report from Commissioners for Enquiring into Fees in Public Offices 1786* (HC 1806, vii).
FOL	*Foreign Office List.* Published annually or biannually from 1852.
Gent. Mag.	*Gentleman's Magazine.*
Jones, *Foreign Office*	Ray Jones, *The nineteenth-century Foreign Office: an administrative history.* London 1971.
Middleton, *Foreign Policy*	C. R. Middleton, *The Administration of British Foreign Policy 1782–1846.* Durham, N. C. 1977.
Officials of the Secretaries of State	*Officials of the Secretaries of State 1660–1782*, comp. J. C. Sainty. London 1973.
Royal Kal.	*Royal Kalendar.*
16th Rept. on Finance	*Sixteenth Report of Select Committee on Finance 1797.* Reports from Committees of House of Commons (15 vols., London 1803) xii, 297–327.

Note on Editorial Method

This volume is designed to make available lists of the officials who served in the Foreign Office between the establishment of the department in 1782 and the year 1870 which witnessed the introduction of the system of open competition for entrants into most departments of the Civil Service. This system was not applied to the Foreign Office until the twentieth century but, to maintain uniformity with the other volumes in this series, the end of the year 1870 has been adhered to as the terminal point for the lists. The material is presented in four parts: an introduction, lists of appointments, periodic lists of officials and an alphabetical list of officials. The purpose of the introduction is to provide a short account of the institutional development of the Foreign Office during the period in order that the various offices and grades may be related to their general context. The lists of appointments give the dates of appointments to these offices and grades. They are preceded by introductory notes which bring together information concerning methods of appointment, remuneration and other relevant matters. The periodic lists enable the complete establishment to be seen at certain significant dates in the development of the Foreign Office.

The alphabetical list is not intended to be a biographical index. Its purpose is confined simply to providing summarised accounts of the offices held by each individual within the Foreign Office during the period. No information has been included unless it is directly relevant to this purpose. Thus dates of death are included only if the individual in question was in office at his death. Appointments to offices outside the Foreign Office have been ignored unless they occasioned, or can reasonably be held to have occasioned, the departure of the official from the Foreign Office. Clerks quite frequently spent periods of time attached to diplomatic missions overseas. Provided that their rank in the Foreign Office was not affected by such service, no mention of it has been made in the alphabetical list. Similarly members of the diplomatic service who temporarily exchanged places with Foreign Office Clerks, or who spent brief periods of training in the Foreign Office before embarking on a mission or in the interval between missions, have been excluded from these lists. In general the accounts of the careers of the 'political' officials, the Secretary of State, his Private Secretary and Précis Writer, and the 'non-permanent' Under Secretaries, have been confined to a simple statement of their periods of service in these offices; information concerning resignations and retirements is provided only in the case of those holding 'permanent' offices. When a Clerk held an additional office within the Foreign Office such as a private secretaryship, which was not directly related to the ordinary course of promotion, the details of his period of service in this additional office have been placed in a separate paragraph. The accounts of the careers of those who were in office at the end of 1870 have not been continued beyond this point.

All references have been concentrated in the alphabetical list. Peers and holders of courtesy titles have been indexed under their titles. In the case of changes of name or status, appropriate cross-references have been inserted. Unless otherwise noted, information concerning peers and baronets has been taken from the *Complete Peerage* (ed. G.E.C. 2nd ed. 13 vols. London 1910–59), the *Complete Baronetage* (ed. G.E.C. 5 vols. Exeter 1900–6) and *Burke's Peerage*.

Certain conventions have been adopted for dating appointments. Where possible the date selected is that of formal entry into office. Thus appointments of Secretaries of State are dated by reference to the day on which they received the seals of office; those of Under Secretaries and Clerks by reference to the letters written in connection with the privilege of franking, where these are available. This information has been supplemented by letters and minutes of appointment issued by the Secretary of State. Where there is no indication of the date of appointment of an official, his period of service is dated by reference to the time during which he received a salary or other remuneration, or, failing this information, by reference to the earliest and latest date at which he is found occupying a particular office. All officials are taken to have remained in office until the appointment of their successors unless there is clear evidence to support the selection of an earlier date.

Introduction

The Foreign Office came into existence in 1782 as a result of the decision to reorganise the business undertaken by the Secretaries of State.[1] Originally there had been two Secretaries of State who shared domestic business. The conduct of foreign affairs, on the other hand, had been divided between them on a geographical basis, an arrangement that had given rise to the designations 'northern' and 'southern' to describe the departments over which they presided. Colonial business formed part of the area of responsibility of the Southern Secretary until 1768 when it was transferred to a third or Colonial Secretary. In 1782 the office of third Secretary of State was abolished. Foreign business was placed exclusively in the hands of one of the remaining Secretaries of State while domestic and colonial business was entrusted to the other. As a consequence the Secretaries of State came to be known as the Foreign and Home Secretaries and their departments as the Foreign and Home Offices.[2]

In institutional terms the Foreign Office took over the staff which had served in the former Northern Department. As constituted in March 1782 it consisted of a Secretary of State, two Under Secretaries, a Chief Clerk and seven other Clerks, the first two of whom were customarily known as Senior Clerks, two Office or Chamber Keepers and a Housekeeper or Necessary Woman.[3] Of these the Secretary of State and the Under Secretaries received salaries from the crown. The Secretary of State, the Under Secretaries, the Chief Clerk and the Office Keepers were also entitled to fixed fees on instruments passing through the office. The Secretary of State was responsible for paying out of his emoluments the salaries of all the Clerks (except the Chief Clerk), the Office Keepers and the Housekeeper. The Clerks also received

[1] For the Foreign Office generally during this period, see especially Middleton, *Foreign Policy* and Jones, *Foreign Office*. Also of value are Sir J. Tilley and S. Gaselee, *The Foreign Office* (London 1933); *The Records of the Foreign Office 1782–1939* (Public Record Office Handbook No. 13, London 1969); and V. Cromwell and Z. S. Steiner, 'The Foreign Office before 1914: a study in resistance', *Studies in the growth of nineteenth-century government*, ed. G. Sutherland (London 1972), 167–94. Information concerning establishment matters generally and authorities for the appointments of most officials were entered in the Chief Clerk's Domestic Books (FO 366/669–74, 449, 675–7; indexed in FO 366/685). Periods of service can be established from the quarterly salary lists 1795–1868 (FO 366/380–5) and various drafts of such lists 1792–1807, 1849–70 (FO 366/1291, 256–8). Detailed accounts of the contingent fund are available for the years 1792–1833 (FO 366/1292) and concise accounts, which rarely name the officials to whom payments were made, for the years 1833–68 (FO 366/228). Full lists of the establishment are included in the *Foreign Office List*, published annually or biannually from 1852.

[2] For the organisation of the secretariat before 1782, see *Officials of the Secretaries of State*, 1–21. The development of the Home Office after 1782 is traced in *Home Office Officials 1782–1870*, comp. J. C. Sainty (London 1975), 1–10.

[3] Several offices, which had been common to the secretariat as a whole before 1782, were retained thereafter. The offices are described and their holders are listed in *Officials of the Secretaries of State*, 21, 43–54. They have therefore been omitted from this volume. The Messengers of the Chamber or King's Messengers have also been excluded. Originally part of the Royal Household under the authority of the Lord Chamberlain, from the later eighteenth century they passed increasingly under the control of the Secretaries of State. For some account of them, see A. V. Wheeler-Holohan, *The History of the King's Messengers* (London 1935).

fixed annual amounts from the Post Office in compensation for the loss of part of the privilege of franking mail.[4] Both Under Secretaries and Clerks customarily received presents on the exchange of treaties with foreign powers. Clerks were permitted to supplement their incomes by serving, in return for a commission, as agents to members of the diplomatic and consular services during their absence abroad.[5]

In the years 1785–6 the offices of the two Secretaries of State were investigated by the Commissioners on Fees. The evidence which they took from the officials of the Foreign Office and which is included in their first report, affords a valuable insight into the manner in which the department was organised at this period.[6] At the time of the Commissioners' investigation only one Under Secretary was serving in the Foreign Office, and one Under Secretary was absent from the Home Office. They therefore concluded that a single Under Secretary, who should be 'stationary' or permanent, was sufficient for the 'necessary official business' of each department. They conceded, however, that a Secretary of State might require the assistance of a second Under Secretary to manage his 'private and confidential business'.[7] This proposed differentiation, which had to a certain extent been foreshadowed by earlier conventions in the two offices, was eventually to form the basis of the distinction between the 'Permanent' and 'Parliamentary' Under Secretaries. The Commissioners recommended the discontinuation of the arrangements under which officials had received their remuneration in uncertain amounts from a variety of different sources and their replacement by a system whereby all allowances, fees and perquisites were carried to a common fund out of which fixed salaries were paid. They also urged the adoption of regular arrangements for retiring pensions and the abolition of the agency system.[8]

It was not until February 1795 that the three Secretaries of State[9] finally submitted their observations on the report of the Commissioners.[10] They rejected the recommendation that there should be one 'permanent' Under Secretary on the ground that there might be circumstances in which a Secretary of State would be justified in making a change in the holders of both these offices. They agreed to the proposal that all officials should be paid fixed salaries from a single source although they stipulated that the number of Clerks and the general level of remuneration should be higher than that originally recommended. They accepted the principle of making proper provision for retiring pensions, but considered that there was nothing improper in the practice of Clerks acting as agents for diplomats. An order in council was thereupon promulgated to give effect to the proposals of the Commissioners as modified by the Secretaries of State. The establishment of the Foreign Office was fixed at one Secretary of State at £6,000, two Under Secretaries at £1,500, a Chief Clerk at £1,000, eleven other Clerks with salaries ranging from £80 to £650, a Private Secretary and a Précis Writer,[11] each with a salary of £300 and two Office Keepers and a Housekeeper, each

[4] *1st Rept. on Fees*, 5–8.

[5] For the treaty presents and the agency system, see Middleton, *Foreign Policy*, 164–9.

[6] *1st Rept. on Fees*, 27–33.

[7] ibid. 10. [8] ibid. 11–16.

[9] A third secretaryship of state with responsibility for war (and subsequently for colonies) was created in 1794. For the development of this office, see *Colonial Office Officials*, comp. J. C. Sainty (London 1976), 1–7.

[10] *16th Rept. on Finance*, 309–11.

[11] A salary of £300, payable out of the contingent fund, had first been made available to a Précis Writer in 1793 (FO 366/1292, payment 3 Nov. 1794).

with £100. All salaries were to be paid by the Chief Clerk out of a fund to which the office fees were to be carried. In the event of the fund falling short, deficiencies were to be met by the civil list.[12] Shortly afterwards the sinecure offices of Collector of State Papers and Translator of the German Language, with salaries of £500 and £300 respectively, were formally included in the Foreign Office establishment.[13]

Various modifications were made to these arrangements in the following two decades. In 1799 the salaries of the Under Secretaries were increased to £2,000 with provision for an increase to £2,500 after three years' service.[14] In February 1801 it was laid down that the salary of the Chief Clerk should increase from £1,000 to £1,250 after five years' service.[15] In the following June an annual allowance of £250 was made available to the First Senior Clerk, S. Rolleston, as Assistant to the Under Secretaries.[16] Rolleston's special duties of superintending and distributing the general business of the office led to his being designated from 1804 Second Chief Clerk with a salary of £1,250.[17] In 1806 the salary of the Translator of the German Language, which had lapsed on the death of its holder in 1802, was revived and divided equally between three officials, two of whom were Clerks on the establishment.[18] The distinct office of Translator of the Spanish, Portuguese, Italian and Danish Languages was created in 1809 with a salary of £300 whereupon the arrangements made in 1806 were discontinued.[19] In January 1809 increasing pressure of business led to the appointment of two additional Clerks.[20] In the following May an arrangement was made for the remuneration of all Clerks to increase in proportion to their length of service, provision being made for £80, £200, £300 and £400 to be added to their salaries after successive periods of five years' service.[21]

In addition to these extra charges upon the fee fund, several new officials were awarded allowances from the contingent fund. An Extra Clerk was employed from 1795.[22] In 1806 a Supernumerary Clerk, who was to succeed to the first vacancy on the establishment, was appointed. The number of such Clerks was increased to three in 1812.[23] Allowances were made available to a Printer in 1800, to a Librarian in 1801, to a Sub-Librarian in 1809 and to a Clerk attached to the Chief Clerk's Department in 1814.[24] All these officials and the Translator were brought within the terms of the order in council of May 1809 which provided for increases in salary after successive periods of five years' service.

[12] See also Civil List Act 1810 (50 Geo. III, c 117, s 9). Following the Civil List Act 1816 (56 Geo. III, c 46) estimates of the amount of the deficiency of the fee fund were laid before the House of Commons and the sums required voted annually. From 1849, when the payment of salaries was transferred to the Paymaster General, the Chief Clerk paid all fees into the Exchequer and the total sum required to defray the charge of the Foreign Office was voted by Parliament.

[13] For these offices, see *Officials of the Secretaries of State*, 49, 54.

[14] Order in council 23 Jan. 1799 (FO 366/671 pp. 101–4).

[15] Order in council 18 Feb. 1801 (ibid. pp. 165–6).

[16] Order in council 16 June 1801 (ibid. pp. 186–8).

[17] Order in council 19 Feb. 1806 (ibid. pp. 298–300).

[18] ibid. p. 303.

[19] Order in council 11 Jan. 1809 (ibid. pp. 362–3).

[20] Order in council 11 Jan. 1809 (ibid. pp. 364–5).

[21] Order in council 10 May 1809 (ibid. pp. 380–2).

[22] FO 366/1292, payment 1 June 1796.

[23] FO 366/671 p. 301; FO 366/672 pp. 45–6.

[24] FO 366/1292, payments 6 Nov. 1800, 10 Feb. 1802, 5 Jan. 1810, 10 Oct. 1814.

The rapid expansion of diplomatic and commercial activity following the cessation of hostilities in 1815 enabled the Foreign Office to resist most of the demands for retrenchment in the immediate post-war period. In 1817, in response to criticism made by the House of Commons, the period of service required by Under Secretaries before they became entitled to the addition of £500 to their salaries was increased from three to seven years.[25] In the same year, on the advancement of S. Rolleston to the office of Chief Clerk, the title and salary of Second Chief Clerk was discontinued.

In 1822, however, parliamentary pressure for economy compelled the Foreign Office in common with other government departments to undertake a comprehensive revision of its establishment.[26] The salaries of the Under Secretaries were fixed at £2,000 without any provision for an increase for length of service. The previous arrangement under which a particular salary had been accorded to each Clerk with provision for increases after successive periods of five years' service was discontinued and replaced by a system according to which the Clerks were divided into classes to which salary scales with regular annual increments were attached. The Chief Clerk retained his special position with a scale ranging from £1,000 to £1,250. The remaining thirteen Clerks were divided into three classes, four Senior or First Class Clerks with a scale ranging from £600 to £800 with provision for the most senior to rise to £900, four Second Class Clerks with a scale ranging from £350 to £545 and five Junior or Third Class Clerks with a scale ranging from £150 to £300. It was laid down that Clerks should rise according to seniority to the head of their class but that they should not be promoted to a higher class without an express appointment by the Secretary of State. The office of Extra Clerk, by this time designated 'Entering and Dispatch Clerk', was abolished and its duties transferred to the Sub-Librarian. The three Supernumerary Clerks then in office were retained, but no decision was taken as to their replacement when vacancies occurred.[27] It was provided that the office of Clerk attached to the Chief Clerk's Department should be abolished on a vacancy when its duties would be performed by one of the established Clerks. The offices of Translator, Précis Writer and Private Secretary were retained with fixed salaries of £300. The Librarian and Sub-Librarian were incorporated into the establishment for the first time, with the same salary scales as the Second Class and Third Class Clerks respectively. The two junior Clerks on the establishment were awarded allowances of £150 as 'Private Secretaries to the Under Secretaries'.[28]

The economies made in 1822 were undermined in the following five years when Canning served as Secretary of State. The work of the department grew rapidly in this period: Central and South America for the first time became a major concern of the Foreign Office; Britain's involvement in the international movement for the suppression of the slave trade, the reorganisation of the consular service and the abolition of the Levant Company created additional responsibilities. Between 1822 and 1827 the number of established Clerks rose from thirteen to twenty-five, the three Supernumerary Clerks of 1822 having been replaced in 1824 by a new grade of Assistant

[25] Order in council 24 July 1817 (FO 366/542 ff. 39–40).

[26] Order in council 28 March 1822 (PC 2/204 pp. 81–8, 103).

[27] FO 366/672 pp. 231–4.

[28] In 1831 Palmerston directed that, as their duties were of a public and not a private nature, the 'Private Secretaries' should henceforth be designated Clerks Assistant to the Under Secretaries (FO 366/673 p. 162). The latter term has been used throughout these lists.

Junior or Fourth Class Clerks with a scale ranging from £100 to £150.[29] On Canning's departure from the office in 1827 the Clerks were graded as: four Senior Clerks, seven Second Class Clerks, six Junior Clerks and eight Assistant Junior Clerks. In the years 1824–7 allowances were awarded to three of the four Senior Clerks for the performance of specific areas of duty. The First and Second Senior Clerks became Superintendents of the newly formed Consular and Slave Trade Departments, and the Third, Superintendent of Foreign Ministers' Accounts.[30] The Fourth Senior Clerk, H. J. Rolleston, continued to receive an allowance, first awarded in 1813, as Superintendent of the Treaty Department.[31] 'Supplementary Clerks'[32] were employed in increasing numbers. The Clerk attached to the Chief Clerk's Department became a permanent feature of the establishment and was awarded in 1823 the same salary scale as the Third Class Clerks and in 1827 the same scale as the Second Class Clerks.[33] Allowances were also made available to three Clerks in the Slave Trade Department and to Clerks attached to the Treaty, Consular and Librarian's Departments.[34] An Assistant Translator was appointed in 1823.[35] In the years 1824–5 and 1826–7 the number of Under Secretaries rose temporarily to three. On both occasions no extra expense was incurred as two of the Under Secretaries shared the salary of one of the offices.[36] Canning informed the Treasury in 1825 that he would soon need the permanent addition of a third Under Secretary[37] but never submitted a concrete proposal to this effect.

The period of growth came to an end when Canning left the Foreign Office and in July 1830 the number of Assistant Junior Clerks was actually reduced from eight to six.[38] The Whig government which took office in November 1830 instigated a modest programme of reform: the office of Assistant Translator was abolished;[39] the salary of the Secretary of State was reduced from £6,000 to £5,000;[40] and the receipt of treaty presents was abolished, compensation being awarded to those officials who suffered by their abolition.[41]

As part of this programme of reform, the position of the Under Secretaries was regulated. Although the three Secretaries of State had rejected in 1795 the recommendations made by the Commissioners on Fees with regard to these offices, by 1831 the practice in both the Home and Colonial Offices conformed closely to their proposals: the standing of one Under Secretary was effectively 'permanent' and

[29] FO 366/672 pp. 375, 381, 429–32; FO 366/673 pp. 24–7, 46. The increases were effected with little resistance from the Treasury and without reference to the Privy Council, the body which since 1795 had approved all changes in the establishment. The last of the increases proposed in December 1826 was in fact not approved by the Treasury until May 1827 by which time Canning himself had become First Lord of the Treasury.

[30] FO 366/672 pp. 429–32; FO 83/40, 4 Dec. 1824; FO 366/673 pp. 28–9, 44–5.

[31] FO 366/672 pp. 68–70.

[32] The Clerks attached at various times to the Chief Clerk's, Treaty, Slave Trade, Librarian's and Consular Departments were not known as 'Supplementary Clerks' until organised into a distinct grade in 1865. The term, therefore, has been avoided wherever possible in these lists.

[33] FO 366/672 pp. 329–30; FO 366/673 p. 36.

[34] FO 96/28/1 ff. 3–4; FO 366/672 pp. 359, 366; FO 366/673 pp. 4, 19, 39–40.

[35] FO 366/672 p. 338.

[36] ibid. pp. 383, 395; FO 366/381.

[37] FO 366/672 pp. 429–32.

[38] FO 366/673 pp. 122–3, 134–5.

[39] ibid. pp. 167, 173.

[40] TM 15 April 1831 (HC 375 p. 2 (1830–1) vii, 494).

[41] FO 366/673 pp. 182–97; Middleton, *Foreign Policy*, 184–5.

unaffected by political change; the second, usually a Member of Parliament, was recognised to be personal to the Secretary of State. In the Foreign Office this practice, although clearly understood, had not hardened into custom. Both Under Secretaries were technically removable at pleasure, and indeed both had been removed on changes of ministry in 1806 and 1807. By 1831, however, J. Backhouse, first appointed by Canning in 1827 and retained by the Whigs in 1830, had probably secured for himself a position of permanence. One Under Secretary was usually a personal connection of the Secretary of State, but since 1808 no Under Secretary had sat in the House of Commons and only two had been members of the House of Lords. Nevertheless in 1831 a Treasury Minute gave formal recognition to the practice adopted in the Home and Colonial Offices and applied it to the Foreign Office. The Under Secretaries in all three departments were for the first time officially designated 'Permanent' and 'Parliamentary' and accorded distinct salaries, £2,000 and £1,500 respectively.[42] However, although the position of the Permanent Under Secretary in the Foreign Office was clearly defined from this point, the tenure of the 'parliamentary' under secretaryship was not invariably associated with membership of either house of parliament until 1852.

Between 1829 and 1838 the number of letters received and sent by the Foreign Office increased from 7,309 to 16,475.[43] As a result the two clerkships reduced in 1830 were restored in 1839. To speed up the slow rate of promotion from the lower to the higher classes the number of Second Class Clerks was increased from seven to ten and the number of Junior Clerks from six to seven while the number of Assistant Junior Clerks was reduced from six to four.[44] The remedy, however, was only partial and the major defect of the establishment as settled by Canning, an unequal relationship between responsibility and remuneration, remained unresolved. In the period after 1822 the Clerks Assistant to the Under Secretaries, whose number was increased to three in 1824 and to four in 1836,[45] became effectively superintendents of the work in the Political Departments of the office.[46] Yet it was not until 1839 that a Clerk Assistant, T. Staveley, rose to the rank of Senior Clerk.[47] The resignation of the Chief Clerk in 1841 provided an opportunity to reorganise the grade of Senior Clerk. The First and Second Senior Clerks, J. Bidwell and Bandinel, Superintendents respectively of the Consular and Slave Trade Departments, were passed over for promotion as they already performed duties of more general interest than the formal financial duties performed by the Chief Clerk. The Third Senior Clerk, Lenox Conyngham, then Superintendent of the Treaty Department, was promoted to the chief clerkship and retained responsibility for the Treaty Department. The number of senior clerkships was increased to six to accommodate the four Clerks Assistant, who now became in name as well as in fact Superintendents of the four Political Departments. The

[42] *Rept. of Select Committee on Reduction of Salaries 1831* (HC 322 p. 6 (1830–1) iii, 450); TM 15 April 1831 (HC 375 p. 2 (1830–1) vii, 494).

[43] FO 366/673 pp. 394–8.

[44] ibid. pp. 394–8, 434.

[45] FO 366/672 p. 394; FO 366/673 p. 314.

[46] The Political Departments were those which dealt with diplomatic business. For the countries allocated to each Department, see *The Records of the Foreign Office 1782–1939* (Public Record Office Handbook No. 13, London 1969), 12–14 and Middleton, *Foreign Policy*, 321–4. From 1852 the members and the responsibilities of the various Departments are fully listed in the *Foreign Office List*.

[47] He replaced Byng who, as Superintendent of Foreign Ministers' Accounts, had performed a duty scarcely commensurate with the rank of Senior Clerk.

maximum salary attached to the grade of Senior Clerk was increased to £1,000.[48]

The opportunity was also taken in 1841 to rationalise the staffing of the subordinate departments.[49] Two Clerks were attached to the Librarian's Department, which since the death in 1839 of the sole Clerk attached to it, had been seriously undermanned. The salaries of the four Clerks attached to the Slave Trade Department, which had previously been paid from the funds voted annually by Parliament to meet the expenses of various commissions for the suppression of the slave trade, were transferred to the fee fund. The Clerk formerly attached to the Treaty Department was placed under the authority of the Chief Clerk. Although the status of all these Clerks was now made permanent, they remained outside the ordinary clerical establishment.

The movement for administrative reform initiated in 1848 affected the Foreign Office as it did all other government departments.[50] Relations between the Foreign Office and the Treasury were frequently strained during this period, but by 1857 reorganisations satisfactory to both departments had been carried out. In November 1848 the Foreign Office agreed to the appointment of a committee of inquiry into its organisation to be composed of Addington, the Permanent Under Secretary, Sir Charles Trevelyan, the Assistant Secretary of the Treasury and W. Gibson Craig, one of the Junior Lords of the Treasury.[51] The three officials met informally from January to April 1850. By April a general understanding had been reached as to the changes necessary and, according to Addington, it was determined that Trevelyan should prepare a report, embodying the changes agreed upon but omitting all reference to the retention or abolition of the agency system upon which no agreement had been reached. Trevelyan's draft report completed by August treated the agency system in detail and was unacceptable to Addington, who by February 1851 had prepared a draft report of his own.[52] By the time of the dissolution of the Treasury commission in February 1852, when the committee was considered to have expired, no report had been approved.

The ill-will thus engendered between the two departments produced an unpleasant exchange of correspondence in 1852 when the Foreign Office applied to the Treasury for the addition of two Assistant Junior Clerks to the Consular Department. The addition was conceded only after a meeting between Malmesbury, the Secretary of State, and Disraeli, the Chancellor of the Exchequer, who agreed to cancel most of the correspondence.[53]

Although unfruitful, the committee's inquiries did provoke widespread discussion of reform within the Foreign Office.[54] The proposals for reorganisation, finally submitted by Clarendon, as Secretary of State, to the Treasury in March 1854 were based on the outcome of these internal discussions.[55] Clarendon noted that between 1841 and 1853 the number of dispatches received and sent had increased

[48] Order in council 21 Aug. 1841 (FO 366/542 ff. 75–80); FO 366/674 pp. 5–12.

[49] Order in council 21 Aug. 1841 (FO 366/542 ff. 75–80).

[50] For the period of administrative reform, see Jones, *Foreign Office*, 22–40.

[51] FO 366/674 pp. 470–3. The following account of the committee's activities is based largely upon Addington's own account submitted to Malmesbury in 1852 (FO 366/449 pp. 38–46).

[52] The unsigned and undated draft report printed in Jones, *Foreign Office*, 148–64, which makes no reference to the agency system, would appear to be that drawn up by Addington.

[53] FO 366/449 pp. 11–47.

[54] ibid. pp. 224–68, 314–39.

[55] ibid. pp. 190–223.

from 24,047 to 35,104 while only two Clerks had been added to the establishment. His principal recommendations were that the number of Political Departments should be increased from four to five, that the number of Senior Clerks should rise accordingly from six to seven and that the remainder of the Clerks should be reclassified. Those Clerks serving as assistants to the Senior Clerks in the seven departments of the office should be formed into a new grade of Assistant Clerks with a scale ranging from £550 to £650. The Junior Clerks would then be divided into three classes corresponding to the old grades of Second Class, Third Class and Fourth Class Clerks. The Slave Trade Department would be staffed by established Clerks. The Treasury objected only to the proposal to create a new class of Assistant Clerks, on the grounds that no such class existed in any other major government department and that the delicate balance between the departments would be destroyed. Instead the Treasury proposed an increase in the number of inferior Clerks and even threw out a suggestion that Copyists might be employed. On this occasion the Treasury view prevailed.[56] In July 1854[57] eight Clerks were added to the establishment which was fixed at seven Senior Clerks, fourteen Second Class Clerks, ten Junior Clerks and six Assistant Junior Clerks. The minimum salary of the Senior Clerks was increased from £600 to £700; all other scales remained unchanged. Shortly afterwards Clarendon secured a minor concession from the Treasury when an annual sum of £300 was made available for distribution amongst the seven Clerks who served as assistants to the Senior Clerks.[58] The Treasury accepted all Clarendon's proposals regarding the subordinate departments. Three Clerks were added to the Librarian's Department. The Treaty Department was removed from the care of the Chief Clerk and placed under a Superintendent with a scale ranging from £600 to £800 and a Clerk, or Assistant, with a scale ranging from £200 to £500. Two Clerks were added to the Chief Clerk's Department. The salary of the Translator was increased to £500.

Increasing pressure of business necessitated the appointment of two additional Junior Clerks and one additional Assistant Junior Clerk in 1856.[59] The reorganisation of the clerical establishment was completed in 1857.[60] The number of Political Departments was increased from five to six and the number of Senior Clerks accordingly increased from seven to eight. The Treasury now accepted the necessity to create a class of Assistant Clerks with a scale ranging from £550 to £650; their number was fixed at nine, two being attached to the Consular Department and one each to the six Political Departments and the Slave Trade Department. The remaining Clerks were reclassified as ten First Class Junior Clerks with a scale ranging from £350 to £545, nine Second Class Junior Clerks with a scale ranging from £150 to £300 and six Third Class Junior Clerks with a scale ranging from £100 to £150. For the first time since Canning's reorganisation of the clerical establishment a balance was struck between responsibility and remuneration and a reasonably rapid rate of promotion from the junior grades was ensured.

In 1858 an Assistant Under Secretary was appointed who in the following year was given a general superintendence of consular affairs.[61] In 1860 one of the two

[56] ibid. pp. 269–303, 305–6.
[57] Order in council 3 July 1854 (FO 366/542 ff. 90–8).
[58] FO 366/449 pp. 311–14, 340–2.
[59] ibid. pp. 450–6.
[60] Order in council 20 March 1857 (FO 366/542 ff. 99–104).
[61] Order in council 11 Jan. 1859 (ibid. ff. 105–11); FO 366/675 pp. 193–7.

Assistant Clerks in the Consular Department was dispensed with and an official described as a 'Supplemental Junior Clerk' was attached to the Department to keep the consular accounts.[62] A Commercial Department was formed at the expense of one of the Political Departments in 1865, and was amalgamated with the Consular Department in the following year. Thereupon the number of Senior Clerks was reduced to seven. Annual allowances of £250 and £100 respectively were made available to the Senior Clerk and the senior of the two Assistant Clerks chosen to serve in the new Department.[63]

The Clerks attached to the Chief Clerk's, Treaty and Librarian's Departments and the 'Supplemental Junior Clerk' in the Consular Department were organised into a uniform grade of Supplementary Clerks in 1865. The Assistant in the Treaty Department and future holders of the offices of Sub-Librarian and First Clerk in the Chief Clerk's Department were placed in a first class with a scale ranging from £400 to £500. The remainder were placed in two further classes with scales ranging from £250 to £360 and £100 to £240 respectively.[64] The reform of accounting procedures in government departments, required under the terms of the Exchequer and Audit Act which came into effect in 1868, necessitated the addition of four Clerks to the Chief Clerk's Department, one of whom was the Supplementary Clerk formerly attached to the Consular Department. A further Clerk was added to the Department in 1869, bringing the total number to eight.[65] The increased accommodation available in the new Whitehall premises to which the Foreign Office moved in 1868 enabled two Supplementary and five Temporary Clerks to be added to the Librarian's Department.[66]

Throughout the nineteenth century, the Foreign Office, because of the high political standing of its Secretaries of State, was in a position to pursue a relatively independent course in matters affecting its establishment. Until 1822 its development was very similar to that of the offices of the other Secretaries of State. Thereafter its establishment grew more quickly than those of the Home and Colonial Offices, but its organisation did not become radically different. On certain issues, in particular the retention of the agency system, an archaic survival from the eighteenth century and opposition to the introduction of Copyists to perform mechanical tasks, the Foreign Office did not conform with the practices adopted in other government departments. But its Secretaries of State rarely abused their privileged status and the Treasury was able to impose some measure of control. In 1870, the end of the period covered by these lists, anomalies still remained. One of them, the agency system, was finally abolished in that year following a sustained and frequently scurrilous press campaign.[67] Conversely a fresh anomaly was created when Clarendon, as Secretary of State, successfully opposed the introduction of open competition for entrants to the Foreign Office at a time when this system was being adopted in almost all other government departments.[68]

[62] FO 366/675 pp. 259–64.
[63] ibid. pp. 535–8; FO 366/676 pp. 122–4, 136–7.
[64] FO 366/675 pp. 543–50; FO 366/676 pp. 5–9.
[65] FO 366/676 pp. 395–404; FO 366/677 pp. 31–50.
[66] FO 366/676 pp. 211–29.
[67] For the abolition of the agency system, see Jones, *Foreign Office*, 97–9.
[68] Candidates for clerkships, nominated by the Secretary of State, had been examined by the Civil Service Commissioners from 1856. For a full account of the entrance system both before and after 1870, see Jones, *Foreign Office*, 41–64.

LISTS OF APPOINTMENTS

Secretary of State 1782–1870

The Secretary of State entered office on receiving the seals from the Sovereign, and took the oath at a meeting of the Privy Council usually held on the same day.[1] His authority lasted until he delivered the seals back to the Sovereign. Originally appointments were formally embodied in letters patent under the great seal granting the office during pleasure. After the appointment of Malmesbury in 1852 this practice was not regularly adopted.

From 1782 to 1795 the Secretary of State received fixed allowances amounting to £5,680 a year together with office fees and other minor perquisites, the total of which varied from year to year.[2] In 1795 a consolidated salary of £6,000 was substituted.[3] In 1831 the salary was reduced to £5,000.[4]

1782	27 March	Fox, Hon. C. J.
1782	10 July	Grantham, Lord
1783	2 April	Fox, Hon. C. J.
1783	19 Dec.	Temple, Earl[5]
1783	23 Dec.	Carmarthen, Marquess of
1791	29 April	Grenville, Lord
1801	20 Feb.	Hawkesbury, Lord
1804	12 May	Harrowby, Lord
1805	11 Jan.	Mulgrave, Lord
1806	7 Feb.	Fox, Hon. C. J.
1806	24 Sept.	Howick, Viscount
1807	25 March	Canning, G.
1809	11 Oct.	Bathurst, Earl
1809	6 Dec.	Wellesley, Marquess
1812	28 Feb.	Castlereagh, Viscount
1822	16 Sept.	Canning, G.
1827	30 April	Dudley and Ward, Viscount
1828	30 May	Aberdeen, Earl of
1830	22 Nov.	Palmerston, Viscount
1834	17 Nov.	Wellington, Duke of
1835	18 April	Palmerston, Viscount
1841	3 Sept.	Aberdeen, Earl of
1846	6 July	Palmerston, Viscount
1851	26 Dec.	Granville, Earl
1852	27 Feb.	Malmesbury, Earl of
1852	28 Dec.	Russell, Lord J.
1853	21 Feb.	Clarendon, Earl of
1858	26 Feb.	Malmesbury, Earl of
1859	18 June	Russell, Lord J.
1865	3 Nov.	Clarendon, Earl of
1866	6 July	Stanley, Lord
1868	9 Dec.	Clarendon, Earl of
1870	6 July	Granville, Earl

[1] In the cases of Grenville (1791) and Granville (1870), where the Foreign Secretary was transferred from another department of state, no fresh oath was taken.

[2] *1st Rept. on Fees*, 5–6, 40–1.

[3] Order in council 27 Feb. 1795 (*16th Rept. on Finance*, 309–11). Following his appointment as Auditor of the Exchequer in 1794 Grenville declined to draw more than £3,200 as Secretary of State so that his total emoluments from office would not exceed £6,000 (Add. MS 59229 f. 143).

[4] TM 15 April 1831 (HC 375 p. 2 (1830–1) vii, 494).

[5] Temporarily held the seals of the Home and Foreign Departments.

Under Secretaries 1782–1870

In 1782 the Foreign Office adopted the convention, which had long operated in the Northern Department, of having two Under Secretaries.[1] With the exceptions of the years 1783–9, when only one Under Secretary held office, and the years 1824–5 and 1826–7, when the number rose temporarily to three, this convention was observed until the end of the period covered by these lists. The modern distinction between the Permanent and Parliamentary Under Secretary, although clearly understood in 1782, evolved gradually in the Foreign Office and hardened into custom at a later date than in the Home and Colonial Offices. The Commissioners on Fees recommended in 1786 that one of the Under Secretaries should have security of tenure or be 'stationary',[2] but their recommendation was rejected by the Secretaries of State on the ground that it placed undue restriction on their freedom of action. The order in council of 1795 which settled the establishment of the office made provision for two undifferentiated Under Secretaries and allowed the Secretaries of State complete freedom of action.[3] It was not until 1831 that the designations 'Permanent' and 'Parliamentary' were first officially applied to the Under Secretaries in the offices of the Secretaries of State and even then the official designations reflected the practice already adopted in the Home and Colonial Offices and merely applied it to the Foreign Office.[4]

From 1831 the position of the Permanent Under Secretary was clearly defined. Before that date both Under Secretaries had been removed simultaneously only on the changes of ministry in February 1806 and March 1807. Eight Under Secretaries had served under more than one Secretary of State, but of these only two, Fraser and Backhouse, served under ministries of radically different political complexions and can confidently be regarded as having attained permanent status.[5]

Before 1831 most Secretaries of State had appointed a personal or political friend to one under secretaryship, but their choice had not been restricted to members of either house of parliament. In the period August 1789–February 1790 both Under Secretaries, Burges and Ryder, were M.P.s.[6] In the years 1782–4 and 1796–1808 one Under Secretary usually sat in the House of Commons.[7] On Bagot's appointment as

[1] For the office generally, see Middleton, *Foreign Policy*, 123–50; E. Jones-Parry, 'Under Secretaries of State for Foreign Affairs, 1782–1855', *English Historical Review*, xlix (1934), 308–20; and C. R Middleton, 'John Backhouse and the origins of the Permanent Undersecretaryship for Foreign Affairs: 1828–1842', *Journal of British Studies*, xiii no. 2 (May 1974), 24–45.

[2] *1st Rept. on Fees*, 10.

[3] Order in council 27 Feb. 1795 (*16th Rept. on Finance*, 309–11).

[4] TM 15 April 1831 (HC 375 p. 2 (1830–1) vii, 494).

[5] Aust claimed in March 1795 that he had been appointed in 1789 '*official* or *resident* Under Secretary, an appointment which he understood to be *comparatively* a permanent one' (Egerton MS 3505, bundle 4).

[6] Ryder was removed in 1790 because it was considered that under a strict interpretation of the Place Act of 1742 only one Under Secretary could sit in the House of Commons (Middleton, *Foreign Policy*, 142). Burges lost his seat in the general election of 1790.

[7] In these periods Sheridan, St. John, Canning, Frere, Hervey, Eliot, Ward, Walpole, Fitzharris and Bagot were M.P.s.

Under Secretary in August 1807, however, he was told by the Secretary of State, Canning, that his duties at the Foreign Office would be too onerous to combine with membership of Parliament.[8] He vacated his seat in the following January. On no further occasion before 1831 did an Under Secretary sit in the House of Commons.[9] Even after the official designation 'parliamentary' had been applied to one under secretaryship in 1831, its tenure was not invariably associated with membership of either house of parliament until 1852.

Until 1831 both Under Secretaries received the same remuneration. From 1782 to 1795 this consisted of a salary of £500 from the civil list together with office fees and other small allowances. While Fraser served as sole Under Secretary in the years 1783–9, he received the emoluments of both offices.[10] In 1795 the salary of each Under Secretary was fixed at £1,500.[11] It was raised to £2,000 in 1799 with provision for an increase to £2,500 after three years' service.[12] In 1817 the period of service required to qualify for the increase was extended to seven years for future occupants of the offices.[13] In 1822 the salary was reduced to £2,000 without any increase for length of service.[14] The salary of one of the offices was shared by two officials in the years 1824–5 and 1826–7.[15] In 1831 a distinction was made between the remuneration of the Permanent and Parliamentary Under Secretary. The salary of the former was fixed at £2,000; that of the latter at £1,500.[16]

The following list has been designed to enable the reader to identify the two Under Secretaries in office at any given moment. Until 1831 no differentiation can be made between the standing of the Under Secretaries. From that date, however, the column on the left of the page contains the names of the Permanent Under Secretaries and that on the right the names of the Parliamentary Under Secretaries. In the alphabetical list of officials the terms 'Permanent' and 'Parliamentary' have been applied to Under Secretaries only from 1831.

1782	27 March	Fraser, W.	1782	27 March	Sheridan, R. B.
			1782	16 July	Maddison, G.
			1783	2 April	St. John, Hon. St. A.
1789	22 Aug.	Burges, J. B.	1789	24 Aug.	Ryder, Hon. D.
			1790	20 Feb.	Aust, G.
1795	16 Oct.	Hammond, G.			
			1796	5 Jan.	Canning, G.
			1799	1 April	Frere, J. H.
			1800	25 Sept.	Fisher, E.

[8] *George Canning and his Friends*, ed. J. Bagot (2 vols., London 1909), i, 238–44.

[9] Howard de Walden and (from 13 Dec. 1826) Clanricarde, however, were members of the House of Lords.

[10] *1st Rept. on Fees*, 6, 27.

[11] Order in council 27 Feb. 1795 (*16th Rept. on Finance*, 309–11).

[12] Order in council 23 Jan. 1799 (FO 366/671 pp. 101–4).

[13] Order in council 24 July 1817 (FO 366/542 ff. 39–40).

[14] Order in council 28 March 1822 (PC 2/204 p. 86). Backhouse, who on his appointment in 1827 also held the office of Receiver General of Excise at a salary of £1,500, was permitted to draw only £500 as Under Secretary. The sum was increased to £1,000 in 1837 in consideration of his long service (FO 366/673 pp. 55–6, 341–7).

[15] FO 366/672 pp. 383, 395; FO 366/381.

[16] TM 15 April 1831 (HC 375 p. 2 (1830–1) vii, 494).

			1801	20 Feb.	Hervey, Lord
			1803	8 Nov.	Arbuthnot, C.
			1804	5 June	Eliot, Hon. W.
			1805	25 Jan.	Ward, R.
1806	20 Feb.	Vincent, Sir F.	1806	20 Feb.	Walpole, Hon. G.
1807	30 March	Hammond, G.	1807	30 March	Fitzharris, Viscount
			1807	19 Aug.	Bagot, Hon. C.
			1809	16 Oct.	Hamilton, W. R.[17]
1809	13 Dec.	Smith, C. C.			
1812	28 Feb.	Cooke, E.			
1817	5 July	Planta, J.			
			1822	30 Jan.	Clanwilliam, Earl of[18]
			1823	6 Jan.	Conyngham, Lord F. N.[19]
			1824	26 May	Conyngham, Lord F. N.; Howard de Walden, Lord,
			1825	17 March	Howard de Walden, Lord
			1826	2 Jan.	Howard de Walden, Lord; Clanricade, Marquess of
1827	23 April	Backhouse, J.			
			1827	12 Aug.	Howard de Walden, Lord
			1828	9 June	Dunglas, Lord
			1830	26 Nov.	Shee, Sir G.[20]
			1834	13 Nov.	Fordwich, Viscount
			1834	15 Dec.	Mahon, Viscount
			1835	15 Aug.	Fox Strangways, Hon. W. T. H[20]
			1840	7 March	Leveson, Lord[20]
			1841	4 Sept.	Canning, Viscount[21]
1842	4 March	Addington, H. U.			
			1846	27 Jan.	Smythe, Hon. G. A. F. P. S.
			1846	6 July	Stanley, Hon. E. J.[22]
			1852	12 Feb.	Layard, A. H.[20]
			1852	18 May	Stanley, Lord
			1852	29 Dec.	Wodehouse, Lord.[21]

[17] Earl of Clanwilliam acted as Under Secretary 17 May 1820–July 1821.
[18] J. Backhouse acted as Under Secretary 26 Oct. 1822–22 Jan. 1823.
[19] Lord Howard de Walden acted as Under Secretary 24 April–26 May 1824.
[20] Not an M.P. while Under Secretary.
[21] Member of the House of Lords.
[22] M.P. from 4 Aug. 1847; member of the House of Lords from 12 May 1848.

1854	10 April	Hammond, E.
1856	4 July	Shelburne, Earl of[21]
1858	26 Feb.	Vesey Fitzgerald, W. R. S.
1859	20 June	Wodehouse, Lord[21]
1861	15 Aug.	Layard, A. H.
1866	6 July	Egerton, E. C.
1868	12 Dec.	Otway, A. J.

[21] See above p. 13.

Assistant Under Secretary 1858–70

In April 1858, when the Parliamentary Under Secretary was hard pressed by parliamentary business and the Permanent Under Secretary was in poor health, Murray, a Senior Clerk, was appointed to the temporary position of Assistant Under Secretary with a monthly allowance of £80 in addition to his salary.[1] Murray's appointment was made permanent in October 1858 at a salary of £1,200.[2] The salary was increased to £1,500 in 1859.[3]

1858	3 Oct.	Murray, J.
1869	3 July	Spring Rice, Hon. T. C. W.
1870	10 Aug.	Russell, O. W. L.

[1] FO 366/675 pp. 17–18.
[2] ibid. pp. 36–9, 45–6; order in council 11 Jan. 1859 (FO 366/542 ff. 105–11).
[3] FO 366/675 pp. 155–6.

Chief Clerks 1782–1870

The office of Chief Clerk, which had been a feature of the Northern Department, formed part of the establishment of the Foreign Office throughout the period. Originally the Chief Clerk, unlike the other Clerks on the establishment, received no salary from the Secretary of State. His remuneration was derived from a fixed proportion of the office fees, £25 from the Irish concordatum fund, an annual allowance of £300 from Post Office funds and a variety of other perquisites and allowances.[1] In 1795 a fixed salary of £1,000 was substituted.[2] In 1801 provision was made for an increase to £1,250 after five years' service.[3] In 1822 the scale was fixed at £1,000 rising by annual increments of £50 to £1,250.[4] Lenox Conyngham was awarded an additional annual allowance of £200 for long service in 1859.[5]

From 1804 the First Senior Clerk, S. Rolleston, was given the title of Chief, or Second Chief, Clerk, and his salary of £650 was increased to £1,250. The duty he had performed as First Senior Clerk, of superintending and distributing the general business of the office, remained unaltered, and he undertook none of the financial and accounting duties normally performed by the Chief Clerk.[6] On Rolleston's appointment to the Chief Clerkship in 1817, the title and salary of Second Chief Clerk lapsed.

CHIEF CLERK

1782	27 March	Sneyd, J.	1841	27 July	Lenox Conyngham, G.
1792	18 April	Bidwell, T.	1866	1 Dec.	Alston, F. B.
1817	28 Sept.	Rolleston, S.			
1824	2 Feb.	Bidwell, T.			

SECOND CHIEF CLERK

1804	10 Aug.	Rolleston, S.

[1] *1st Rept. on Fees*, 6, 27–8.
[2] Order in council 27 Feb. 1795 (*16th Rept. on Finance*, 309–11).
[3] Order in council 18 Feb. 1801 (FO 366/671 pp. 165–6).
[4] Order in council 28 March 1822 (PC 2/204 p. 86).
[5] FO 366/675 pp. 160–2.
[6] Order in council 19 Feb. 1806 (FO 366/671 pp. 298–300).

Clerks 1782–1822

Until 1795 no fixed convention governed the number of Clerks appointed by the Secretary of State. On its formation in 1782 the Foreign Office contained, in addition to the Chief Clerk, seven established Clerks.[1] The number was increased to eight in July 1782, to nine in 1783 and to ten in 1790.[2] From 1793 the number fluctuated until it was fixed at eleven in 1795.[3] In 1804 the number effectively fell to ten when the First Senior Clerk was given the title of Second Chief Clerk.[4] The appointment of two additional Clerks was authorised in 1809.[5] The title of Second Chief Clerk was discontinued in 1817 and the number of Clerks rose to the permitted maximum of thirteen. An unsalaried Supernumerary Clerk held office, February 1801–February 1802 and September 1802–January 1803.

As had been the practice in the Northern Department, the term 'Senior Clerk' was applied until 1804 to the two most senior Clerks and from 1804 until 1822 to the three most senior Clerks in the office.[6] The term, however, has not been adopted in these lists until it was applied to a distinct grade in 1822, when the Clerks were divided into three classes of Senior, Second Class and Junior.

Between 1782 and 1795 the Clerks received their remuneration in the form of salaries from the Secretary of State, allowances from the Post Office and various perquisites.[7] In the latter year they were provided with consolidated salaries from the fee fund, receiving in order of seniority £650, £450, £300, £200, £160, £140, £130, £120, £110, £100 and £80.[8] The two Clerks added to the establishment in 1809 were each accorded salaries of £80.[9] In 1809 provision was made for the salary of each Clerk to be increased according to length of service, the amounts being £80 after five years, £200 after ten years, £300 after fifteen years and £400 after twenty years.[10]

1782	27 March	Broughton, B.
1782	27 March	Aust, G.
1782	27 March	Bidwell, T.
1782	27 March	Carter, R.
1782	27 March	Jenkins, J. W.
1782	27 March	Money, W.
1782	27 March	Manby, J.
1782	16 July	Hinchliffe, J.
1783	31 July	Rolleston, S.
1784	5 July	Moore, F.
1787	12 Jan.	Jackson, F. J.
1788	22 April	Broughton, C. R.

[1] FO 366/669, pt. i, p. 65.

[2] ibid. pt. ii, pp. 5, 47; FO 366/670 p. 61.

[3] Order in council 27 Feb. 1795 (*16th Rept. on Finance*, 309–11).

[4] See p. 16.

[5] Order in council 11 Jan. 1809 (FO 366/671 pp. 364–5).

[6] It was used invariably in the published lists of the establishment and in the Foreign Office quarterly salary book 1795–1822 (FO 366/380).

[7] *1st Rept. on Fees*, 6–7, 29–32.

[8] Order in council 27 Feb. 1795 (*16th Rept. on Finance*, 309–11). The salary of £650 was not made available to a Clerk in the years 1804–17 but formed part of the salary of the Second Chief Clerk.

[9] Order in council 11 Jan. 1809 (FO 366/671 pp. 364–5).

[10] Order in council 10 May 1809 (ibid. pp. 380–2).

1788	17 Oct.	Hay, J. W.
1790	20 Oct.	Bidwell, T.
1790	20 Oct.	Warren, C.
1792	2 Aug.	Taylor, H.
1793	27 Sept.	Taylor, W. W.
1793	27 Sept.	Taylor, B.
1794		Flint, C. W.
1795	5 Jan.	Cockburn, A.
1796	21 April	Wynn, T. E.
1797	18 Aug.	Casamajor, J.
1798	5 July	Noel, C. N.
1799	1 April	Williams Wynn, H. W.
1799	1 April	Bidwell, J.
1799	5 April	Bandinel, J.
1801	23 Jan.	Byng, F. G.
1801	1 Feb.	Hoppner, R. B.
1802	17 Feb.	Rolleston, H. J.[11]
1803	5 Jan.	Planta, J.[12]
1805	18 Oct.	Graham, D.
1809	5 Jan.	Jackson, J.
1809	20 Jan.	Turner, W.
1814	5 July	Scheener, E.
1817	5 July	Lenox Conyngham, G.
1817	5 July	Bankhead, C.
1817	28 Sept.	Staveley, T.
1818	5 July	Parish, W.

[11] Served as unsalaried Supernumerary Clerk from 1 Feb. 1801.
[12] Served as unsalaried Supernumerary Clerk from 27 Sept. 1802.

Supernumerary Clerks 1806–24

In 1806 J. Jackson, who had served since 1799 as an Extra Clerk, was granted the franking privileges normally enjoyed by established Clerks, and appointed a Supernumerary Clerk, to succeed to the next vacancy on the establishment.[1] On succeeding to the establishment in 1809, he was replaced and in 1812 the number of such Clerks was increased to three.[2] In 1819 Joseph Cade was employed in the Foreign Office without salary until he should succeed to the first vacancy as Third Supernumerary Clerk.[3] In 1824 the three Supernumerary Clerks then in office were appointed to the establishment, and the grade was replaced by that of Assistant Junior Clerk.[4]

Until 1822 all Supernumerary Clerks received a basic salary of £100, payable from the contingent fund.[5] After five years' service they became eligible, in common with the established Clerks, to receive an increase in salary of £80.[6] In 1822 their salaries were transferred to the fee fund, and fixed at £100 rising by annual increments of £10 to £150.[7]

1806	27 Jan.	Jackson, J.
1809	5 Aug.	Scheener, E.
1812	10 Nov.	Lenox Conyngham, G.
1812	10 Nov.	Marshall, S. G.
1814	24 Dec.	Bankhead, C.
1814	24 Dec.	Staveley, T.
1817	15 Aug.	Parish, W.
1817	15 Aug.	Passmore, U.
1817	29 Nov.	Ward, T. L.
1818	4 July	McMahon, E.
1823	12 Nov.	Stapleton, A. G.
1823	12 Nov.	Milbanke, J. R.
1824	13 Feb.	Liddell, Hon. T.
1824	13 Feb.	Mellish, R. C.
1824	13 Feb.	Mildmay, H. C. St. J.

1 FO 366/671 pp. 284, 301.
2 ibid. pp. 392–3; FO 366/672 pp. 45–6.
3 FO 366/672 p. 175. In fact he left the Foreign Office before a vacancy arose.
4 ibid. pp. 375, 381.
5 FO 366/671 pp. 301, 393; FO 366/672 pp. 45–6.
6 FO 366/672 pp. 206, 316.
7 Order in council 28 March 1822 (PC 2/204 p. 86).

Senior Clerks 1822–70

Although the term 'Senior Clerk' had been used since 1782 to describe the two or three most senior Clerks on the establishment, it was not until 1822 that it was applied to a distinct grade.[1] In that year provision was made for four Senior, or First Class, Clerks.[2] In 1841 the number was increased to six, two of whom were to serve as Superintendents of the Consular and Slave Trade Departments, and four of whom were to assist the Under Secretaries in superintending the four Political Departments of the office.[3] Following the creation of additional Political Departments, the number was increased to seven in 1854 and to eight in 1857.[4] In 1866 when the Commercial Department (formed in 1865 at the expense of a Political Department) was amalgamated with the Consular Department, the number was reduced to seven.[5] From 1855 new entrants to the grade were required to serve a period of one year's probation.[6]

In 1822 the first of the Senior Clerks was awarded a salary of £700 rising by annual increments of £20 to £900 while the remainder were granted salaries of £600 rising by annual increments of £20 to £800.[7] In 1841 a scale of £600 rising by annual increments of £25 to £1,000 was provided for the whole grade. All the Senior Clerks in office following the reorganisation of 1841 held annual allowances of varying amounts granted to them before 1841 for the performance of specific duties. They were allowed to retain what they then held. But those holding allowances greater than £200 were not allowed to draw salaries as Senior Clerks greater than £800; while those holding allowances of less than £200 were allowed to advance beyond £800 until such time as their salaries and allowances amounted in total to £1,000.[8] The minimum salary attached to the grade was increased to £700 in 1854.[9]

1822	28 March	Broughton, C. R.
1822	28 March	Bidwell, T.
1822	28 March	Bidwell, J.
1822	28 March	Bandinel, J.
1824	5 Jan.	Byng, Hon. F. G.
1824	5 Jan.	Rolleston, H. J.
1834	16 May	Lenox Conyngham, G.
1839	5 April	Staveley, T.
1841	16 Aug.	Ward, T. L.
1841	21 Aug.	Mellish, R. C.
1841	21 Aug.	Hammond, E.
1845	13 Dec.	Oom, A. K.
1851	1 Oct.	Murray, J.
1854	10 April	Forster, H. F.
1854	1 July	Coles, A. L.

[1] See p. 17.
[2] Order in council 28 March 1822 (PC 2/204 p. 86).
[3] Order in council 21 Aug. 1841 (FO 366/542 ff. 75–80).
[4] Orders in council 3 July 1854 (ibid. ff. 90–8) and 20 March 1857 (ibid. ff. 99–104).
[5] FO 366/676 pp. 122–4, 136–7.
[6] FO 366/449 p. 369.
[7] Order in council 28 March 1822 (PC 2/204 p. 86).
[8] Order in council 21 Aug. 1841 (FO 366/542 ff. 75–80).
[9] Order in council 3 July 1854 (ibid. ff. 90–8).

1855	1 Jan.	Wylde, W. H.[10]	1860	1 Jan.	Morier, G.
1856	1 Jan.	Wellesley, R. G.	1860	22 Aug.	Staveley, T. G.
1857	13 March	Spring Rice, Hon. T. C. W.	1863	2 Aug.	Pennell, J. C.
			1865	4 June	Hole, J. B.
1857	1 April	Alston, F. B.	1866	1 Dec.	Woodford, J. W. G.
1859	1 Jan.	Wylde, W. H.[11]	1868	1 Jan.	Gifford, Hon. E. S.
1859	1 April	Bidwell, J.	1869	3 July	Vivian, Hon. H. C.

[10] Probationary.
[11] Reappointed.

Second Class Clerks 1822–57

The grade of Second Class Clerk was created in March 1822 when provision was made for four such Clerks with salaries of £350 rising by annual increments of £15 to £545.[1] In May 1822 two supernumeraries were added to the grade.[2] In 1824 the number was fixed at six with no supernumeraries.[3] It was raised to seven in 1827, to ten in 1839 and to fourteen in 1854.[4] In 1857 the Second Class Clerks then in office were distributed amongst the two newly created grades of Assistant Clerk and First Class Junior Clerk.

1822	28 March	Byng, Hon. F. G.
1822	28 March	Rolleston, H. J.
1822	28 March	Jackson, J.
1822	28 March	Turner, W.
1822	29 May	Scheener, E.[5]
1822	29 May	Lenox Conyngham, G.[5]
1823	10 Oct.	Scheener, E.
1824	5 Jan.	Lenox Conyngham, G.
1824	5 Jan.	Bankhead, C.
1824	5 April	Staveley, T.
1824	5 April	Ward, T. L.
1826	5 Jan.	McMahon, E.
1827	5 Jan.	Stapleton, A. G.
1827	5 July	Mellish, R. C.
1830	5 July	Mildmay, H. C. St. J.
1830	5 July	Hammond, E.
1834	16 May	Turner, A.
1839	5 April	Oom, A. K.
1839	5 July	Stopford, W. B.
1839	5 July	Murray, J.
1839	5 July	Scott, C.
1841	16 Aug.	Forster, H. F.
1841	21 Aug.	Dawkins, C. G. A.
1841	21 Aug.	Taylor, B.
1841	29 Oct.	Blackburn, J. E.
1843	11 April	Huskisson, W. M.
1843	7 Aug.	Coles, A. L.
1844	9 March	Backhouse, G. C.
1845	12 Dec.	Wylde, W. H.
1846	6 Jan.	Wellesley, R. G.
1846	26 June	Spring Rice, Hon. T. C. W.
1849	14 Jan.	Alston, F. B.
1851	1 Oct.	Ponsonby, Hon. S. C. B.
1851	18 Nov.	Hole, J. B.
1852	14 Dec.	Bidwell, J.
1852	16 Dec.	Morier, G.
1854	10 April	Staveley, T. G.
1854	1 July	Pennell, J. C.
1854	1 July	Woodford, J. W. G.
1854	1 July	Gifford, Hon. E. S.
1854	1 July	Synge, W. W. F.
1854	1 July	Cavendish, F. W. H.
1855	1 Jan.	Wolff, H. D.
1856	1 Jan.	Wylde, W. H.[6]
1856	1 Dec.	Vivian, Hon. H. C.
1857	13 March	Dashwood, J. E. B.

[1] Order in council 28 March 1822 (PC 2/204 p. 86).
[2] FO 366/672 pp. 266–7.
[3] ibid. pp. 375, 381; FO 366/381.
[4] FO 366/673 pp. 24–7, 46, 394–8, 434; order in council 3 July 1854 (FO 366/542 ff. 90–8).
[5] Supernumerary.
[6] Reappointed.

Junior Clerks 1822–57

The grade of Junior, or Third Class, Clerk was created in 1822 when provision was made for five such Clerks with salaries of £150 rising by annual increments of £15 to £300.[1] The number was increased to six in 1824 and to seven in 1825; reduced to six in 1827; and again increased to seven in 1839, to ten in 1854 and to twelve in 1856.[2] In 1857 the Junior Clerks then in office were distributed amongst the two newly created grades of First Class Junior Clerk and Second Class Junior Clerk.

1822	28 March	Scheener, E.
1822	28 March	Lenox Conyngham, G.
1822	28 March	Bankhead, C.
1822	28 March	Staveley, T.
1822	28 March	Parish, W.
1823	10 Oct.	Ward, T. L.
1823	10 Oct.	McMahon, E.
1824	5 Jan.	Stapleton, A. G.
1824	5 Jan.	Milbanke, J. R.
1824	5 April	Liddell, Hon. T.
1824	5 April	Mellish, R. C.
1824	5 April	Mildmay, H. C. St. J.
1825	5 Jan.	Hammond, E.
1826	5 Jan.	Turner, A.
1826	5 April	Oom, A. K.
1826	5 July	Hervey, Lord W.
1827	5 July	Lowth, G.
1828	5 Jan.	Stopford, W. B.
1830	5 July	Adams, W. P.
1830	5 July	Murray, J.
1834	16 May	Molyneux, Hon. F. G.
1834	17 Nov.	Scott, C.
1835	10 Oct.	Forster, H. F.
1838	5 April	Dawkins, C. G. A.
1839	5 April	Taylor, B.
1839	5 July	Cowper, Hon. C. S.
1839	5 July	Blackburn, J. E.
1839	5 July	Huskisson, W. M.
1839	5 July	Coles, A. L.
1839	22 Nov.	Backhouse, G. C.
1841	16 Aug.	Wylde, W. H.
1841	21 Aug.	Wellesley, R. G.
1841	21 Aug.	Spring Rice, Hon. T. C. W.
1841	29 Oct.	Alston, F. B.
1843	11 April	Paget, A. B.
1843	7 Aug.	Ponsonby, Hon. S. C. B.
1844	9 March	Hole, J. B.
1845	12 Dec.	Bidwell, J.
1846	6 Jan.	Morier, G.
1846	26 June	Staveley, T. G.
1846	26 June	Pennell, J. C.
1849	14 Jan.	Woodford, J. W. G.
1851	1 Oct.	Gifford, Hon. E. S.
1851	18 Nov.	Synge, W. W. F.
1852	14 Dec.	Cavendish, F. W. H.
1852	16 Dec.	Wolff, H. D.
1854	10 April	Vivian, Hon. H. C.
1854	1 July	Dashwood, J. E. B.
1854	1 July	Cowell, A. K.
1854	1 July	Kennedy, C. M.
1854	1 July	Lister, T. V.
1854	1 July	Anderson, H. P.
1854	1 July	Abbott, C. S. A.
1854	1 Oct.	Currie, P. H. W.
1854	1 Oct.	Vernon, G. R.
1855	1 Jan.	Crichton Stuart, H.
1856	1 Dec.	Stephens, F. S. M.
1856	1 Dec.	Hervey, H. A. W.
1856	1 Dec.	Clarke Jervoise, H. S. C.
1857	13 March	Walsham, J.

[1] Order in council 28 March 1822 (PC 2/204 p. 86). The number fell to three in May 1822 when two of the Junior Clerks were appointed Supernumerary Second Class Clerks.

[2] FO 366/672 pp. 375, 381; FO 366/381; FO 366/394, 4 April 1825; FO 366/673 pp. 24–7, 46, 394–8, 434; order in council 3 July 1854 (FO 366/542 ff. 90–8); FO 366/449 pp. 450–6.

Assistant Junior Clerks 1824–57

The grade of Assistant Junior, or Fourth Class, Clerk was created in 1824 when provision was made for three such Clerks with salaries of £100 rising by annual increments of £10 to £150.[1] The number was increased to four in 1826 and to eight in 1827; reduced to six in 1830 and to four in 1839; and again increased to six in 1852 and to seven in 1856.[2] In 1826, 1839 and 1854 additional appointments were made to the grade before formal approval was given to increases in the size of the establishment. Although technically supernumeraries, Clerks so appointed have been classed as established from the dates of their appointment by the Secretary of State. In 1857 the Assistant Junior Clerks then in office were distributed amongst the two newly created grades of Second Class Junior Clerk and Third Class Junior Clerk.

1824	30 April	Hammond, E.
1824	30 April	Turner, A.
1824	30 April	Oom, A. K.
1825	21 Jan.	Hervey, Hon. W.
1826	5 Jan.	Lowth, G.
1826	5 Jan.	Stopford, W. B.
1826	5 April	Adams, W. P.
1826	20 Sept.	Robinson, H. S.
1826	11 Nov.	Murray, J.
1827	23 April	Ryder, Hon. F. D.
1827	23 April	Edwardes, Hon. R.
1827	23 April	Wrangham, D. C.
1827	31 Aug.	Molyneux, Hon. F. G.
1828	11 Jan.	Scott, C.
1829	27 Aug.	Forster, H. F.
1831	26 April	Dawkins, C. G. A.
1832	17 Aug.	Sulivan, S. H.
1834	29 Oct.	Taylor, B.
1834	14 Nov.	Cowper, Hon. C. S.
1834	17 Nov.	Blackburn, J. E.
1834	17 Nov.	Huskisson, W. M.
1835	2 Nov.	Coles, A. L.
1838	24 May	Backhouse, G. C.
1839	5 April	Wylde, W. H.
1839	22 Nov.	Wellesley, R. G.
1839	15 Dec.	Spring Rice, Hon. T. C. W.
1839	15 Dec.	Alston, F. B.
1841	21 Aug.	Paget, A. B.
1841	21 Aug.	Ponsonby, Hon. S. C. B.
1841	21 Aug.	Hole, J. B.
1842	5 Jan.	Bidwell, J.
1843	26 Aug.	Morier, G.
1843	26 Aug.	Staveley, T. G.
1844	9 March	Pennell, J. C.
1845	12 Dec.	Woodford, J. W. G.
1846	5 Feb.	Gifford, Hon. E. S.
1846	26 June	Synge, W. W. F.
1846	26 June	Hope Johnstone, J.
1848	9 May	Cavendish, F. W. H.
1849	14 Jan.	Wolff, H. D.
1851	1 Oct.	Townshend, J. V. S.
1851	18 Nov.	Vivian, Hon. H. C.
1852	14 Aug.	Dashwood, J. E. B.
1852	26 Sept.	Cowell, A. K.
1852	14 Dec.	Astley, H. F. L.
1852	17 Dec.	Kennedy, C. M.
1853	23 Aug.	Lister, T. V.
1854	1 April	Anderson, H. P.
1854	10 April	Abbott, C. S. A.

[1] FO 366/672 pp. 375, 381.

[2] ibid. pp. 429–32; FO 366/673 pp. 24–7, 46, 122–3, 134–5, 394–8, 434; FO 366/449 pp. 11–17, 47, 450–6.

1854	10 April	Currie, P. H. W.	1854	1 Oct.	Walsham, J.
1854	7 May	Vernon, G. R.	1854	22 Dec.	Owen, W.
1854	7 May	Crichton Stuart, H.	1855	28 Jan.	Eliot, Hon. H. C.
1854	7 May	Stephens, F. S. M.	1857	12 Jan.	Buckley, V.
1854	7 May	Hervey, H. A. W.	1857	23 Jan.	Crawford, O. J. F.
1854	16 Aug.	Clarke Jervoise, H. S. C.	1857	21 Feb.	Farquharson, J. A.
			1857	31 March	Warburton, J. W.

Assistant Clerks 1857–70

The grade of Assistant, or Second Class, Clerk was created in 1857 when provision was made for nine such Clerks with salaries of £550 rising by annual increments of £20 to £650.[1] The number was reduced to eight in 1860.[2] The salary was paid only to those Clerks actually performing the duty of assistant to a Senior Clerk in one of the departments into which the work of the office was divided. Thus an Assistant Clerk serving as Private Secretary to the Secretary of State or as Précis Writer, while retaining his rank as an Assistant Clerk, received the salary only of a First Class Junior Clerk, and the First Class Junior Clerk acting in his place received the salary of an Assistant Clerk.[3] In 1866 an additional annual allowance of £100 was made available to the senior of the two Assistant Clerks attached to the newly created Commercial and Consular Department.[4]

1857	1 April	Wylde, W. H.
1857	1 April	Ponsonby, Hon. S. C. B.
1857	1 April	Hole, J. B.
1857	1 April	Bidwell, J.
1857	1 April	Morier, G.
1857	1 April	Staveley, T. G.
1857	1 April	Pennell, J. C.
1857	1 April	Woodford, J. W. G.
1857	1 April	Gifford, Hon. E. S.
1857	7 Dec.	Synge, W. W. F.
1859	1 Jan.	Cavendish, F. W. H.
1859	1 April	Wolff, H. D.
1859	1 June	Vivian, Hon. H. C.
1860	1 Jan.	Dashwood, J. E. B.
1862	1 Jan.	Cowell Stepney, A. K.
1863	2 Aug.	Kennedy, C. M.
1863	1 Oct.	Lister, T. V.
1865	4 June	Anderson, H. P.
1866	1 Dec.	Abbott, C. S. A.
1868	1 Jan.	Currie, P. H. W.
1869	3 July	Stephens, F. S. M.

1 Order in council 20 March 1857 (FO 366/542 ff. 99–104).
2 FO 366/675 pp. 259–64.
3 FO 366/676 pp. 409–15.
4 ibid. pp. 122–4, 136–7.

First Class Junior Clerks 1857–70

The grade of First Class Junior, or Third Class, Clerk was created in 1857 when provision was made for ten such Clerks with salaries of £350 rising by annual increments of £15 to £545.[1]

1857	1 April	Synge, W. W. F.	1859	1 June	Stephens, F. S. M.
1857	1 April	Cavendish, F. W. H.	1859	28 July	Hervey, H. A. W.
1857	1 April	Wolff, H. D.	1860	1 Jan.	Clarke Jervoise, H. S. C.
1857	1 April	Vivian, Hon. H. C.			
1857	1 April	Dashwood, J. E. B.	1862	1 Jan.	Owen, W.
1857	1 April	Cowell, A. K.	1863	2 Aug.	Eliot, Hon. H. C.
1857	1 April	Kennedy, C. M.	1863	1 Oct.	Buckley, V.
1857	1 April	Lister, T. V.	1865	4 June	Crawford, O. J. F.
1857	1 April	Anderson, H. P.	1866	1 Dec.	Warburton, J. W.
1857	1 April	Abbott, C. S. A.	1867	3 Jan.	Farquharson, J. A.
1857	7 Dec.	Currie, P. H. W.	1868	1 Jan.	Lowry Corry, A. H.
1859	1 Jan.	Vernon, G. R.	1869	3 July	Sanderson, T. H.
1859	1 April	Crichton Stuart, H.	1870	30 June	Meade, Hon. R. H.

[1] Order in council 20 March 1857 (FO 366/542 ff. 99–104).

Second Class Junior Clerks 1857–70

The grade of Second Class Junior, or Fourth Class, Clerk was created in 1857 when provision was made for nine such Clerks with salaries of £150 rising by annual increments of £10 to £300.[1]

1857	1 April	Currie, P. H. W.	1860	1 Jan.	Russell, R.
1857	1 April	Vernon, G. R.	1862	1 Jan.	Mitford, A. B.
1857	1 April	Crichton Stuart, H.	1863	2 Aug.	Sanderson, T. H.
1857	1 April	Stephens, F. S. M.	1863	1 Oct.	Meade, Hon. R. H.
1857	1 April	Hervey, H. A. W.	1864	7 Sept.	Cockerell, W. A.
1857	1 April	Clarke Jervoise, H. S. C.	1865	4 June	Bergne, J. H. G.
			1866	1 Dec.	Hughes, L. W. H.
1857	1 April	Walsham, J.	1867	3 Jan.	Brabazon, Lord
1857	1 April	Owen, W.	1867	2 June	Bertie, Hon. F. L.
1857	1 April	Eliot, Hon. H. C.	1868	1 Jan.	Dallas, G. E.
1857	7 Dec.	Buckley, V.	1868	7 March	Robertson, C. B.
1859	1 Jan.	Crawford, O. J. F.	1868	8 June	Howard, Hon. K.
1859	1 April	Warburton, J. W.	1869	3 July	Barrington, Hon. B. E. E.
1859	1 June	Farquharson, J. A.			
1859	28 July	Lowry Corry, A. H.	1870	30 June	Langley, H. F. J.
1860	1 Jan.	Alexander, R. Du P.	1870	30 Dec.	Hill, C. L.

[1] Order in council 20 March 1857 (FO 366/542 ff. 99–104).

Third Class Junior Clerks 1857–70

The grade of Third Class Junior, or Fifth Class, Clerk was created in 1857 when provision was made for six such Clerks with salaries of £100 rising by annual increments of £10 to £150.[1]

1857	1 April	Buckley, V.
1857	1 April	Crawford, O. J. F.
1857	1 April	Warburton, J. W.
1857	1 April	Farquharson, J. A.
1857	14 May	Lowry Corry, A. H.
1857	4 July	Alexander, R. Du P.
1858	22 Feb.	Russell, R.
1859	29 Jan.	Mitford, A. B.
1859	23 April	Sanderson, T. H.
1859	1 June	Meade, Hon. R. H.
1859	16 Aug.	Vyner, R. A.
1860	19 Jan.	Cavendish, Hon. H. A.
1860	27 Jan.	Cockerell, W. A.
1861	14 March	Bergne, J. H. G.
1862	15 March	Hughes, L. W. H.
1863	30 July	Brabazon, Lord
1863	6 Nov.	Bertie, Hon. F. L.
1863	1 Dec.	Dallas, G. E.
1865	30 Jan.	Robertson, C. B.
1865	20 June	Howard, Hon. K.
1867	7 Feb.	Barrington, Hon. B. E. E.
1867	11 Feb.	Langley, H. F. J.
1867	3 Sept.	Hill, C. L.
1868	18 March	Northcote, H. S.
1868	25 May	Wylde, E. W.
1868	5 Aug.	Taylor, B. P. B.
1870	23 Aug.	Nicolson, A.
1870	3 Dec.	Lee, H. A.
1870	30 Dec.	Villiers, Hon. F. H.

[1] Order in council 20 March 1857 (FO 366/542 ff. 99–104).

Extra Clerks 1795–1854

Because of the confidential nature of the business in the Foreign Office, most Secretaries of State were unwilling to employ Extra Clerks or Copyists. Certain Extra Clerks, however, were drawn into the substantial work of the office and are listed below.

One Extra Clerk was employed in the years 1795–1822. The salary, payable out of the contingent fund, was fixed at £70 in 1795 and increased to £80 in 1800 and to £100 in 1801.[1] Bartlett, who was appointed an Extra Clerk in 1806, was attached to the Second Chief Clerk and became known in the course of time as 'Entering and Dispatch Clerk'.[2] His salary was increased to £150 in 1809.[3] In 1811 he was allowed to share in the benefits of the order in council of May 1809 which provided increases of £80, £200, £300 and £400 after successive periods of five years' service.[4] As it was thought that the designation 'Extra Clerk' implied that Bartlett was 'removeable at pleasure', the Treasury approved in 1819 the Foreign Office's suggestion that Bartlett should be considered as 'permanently attached', and that his salary should be increased to £200.[5] On Bartlett's appointment to a consulship in 1822 the office of Entering and Dispatch Clerk was discontinued and its duties transferred to the Sub-Librarian.[6]

An unsalaried Extra Clerk was employed in the years 1828–31.[7] In 1837 a salary of £100, payable out of the contingent fund, was again made available to an Extra Clerk.[8] The number of such Clerks was increased to two in 1840.[9] On the reorganisation of the office in 1841 the two Extra Clerks were appointed to the establishment and not replaced. In the years 1850–1 and in April 1854 an Extra, or Probationary, Clerk was employed at a salary of £100.[10]

1795	*c.* Oct.	Dickens, J.
1798	5 July	Bidwell, J.
1799	5 April	Jackson, J.
1806	7 Feb.	Bartlett, R.
1828	11 Jan.	Forster, H. F.
1829	27 Aug.	Dawkins, C. G. A.
1837	13 Dec.	Browne, J. H. T. T.
1838	14 March	Wylde, W. H.
1839	10 May	Wellesley, R. G.
1840	17 March	Paget, A. B.
1840	29 Oct.	Ponsonby, Hon. S. C. B.
1850	18 June	Townshend, J. V. S.
1854	1 April	Abbott, C. S. A.

[1] FO 366/1292, payments 1 June 1796, 25 Oct. 1800, 6 July 1801.
[2] FO 366/671 p. 301.
[3] ibid. p. 388.
[4] FO 366/672 pp. 28–9, 32, 112, 115.
[5] ibid. pp. 170–1.
[6] ibid. pp. 231–4; order in council 28 March 1822 (PC 2/204 p. 86).
[7] FO 366/673 pp. 66, 102.
[8] ibid. p. 336.
[9] ibid. p. 505.
[10] FO 366/674 p. 496; FO 366/449 p. 154.

Clerks attached to Chief Clerk's Department 1814–70

In 1814 a salary of £80 was made available to H. D. Scott, a Clerk attached exclusively to the Chief Clerk's Department.[1] After he had completed five years' service his salary was increased to £160.[2] In 1822 it was provided that the office should be abolished on a vacancy when its duties would be performed by one of the established Clerks. The salary, transferred from the contingent fund to the fee fund, was to remain fixed at £160.[3] In 1823, however, this decision was reversed and Scott's salary was assimilated to that of the Junior Clerks: £150 rising by annual increments of £15 to £300.[4] In 1827 the salary was raised to £350 rising by annual increments of £15 to £545.[5] An additional personal allowance of £100 was made available to Scott in 1845.[6] In 1854 the number of Clerks was increased to three. Future holders of the office of First Clerk, which was still filled by Scott, were to receive a salary of £200 rising by annual increments of £15 to £400. The salaries of the Second and Third Clerks were fixed at £100 rising by annual increments of £10 to £200.[7] In 1865 the Second and Third Clerks were placed in the new grade of Third Class Supplementary Clerk with salaries of £100 rising by annual increments of £10 to £240. The regrading of the office of First Clerk was delayed until Scott's retirement in 1866 when his successor, Ayers, was placed in the grade of First Class Supplementary Clerk with a salary of £400 rising by annual increments of £15 to £500.[8] The Department was reorganised in 1868 when reforms in accounting procedure, required under the terms of the Exchequer and Audit Act, came into effect. The number of Clerks was increased to seven, consisting of two First Class, two Second Class and three Third Class Supplementary Clerks. The First Clerk then serving in the Chief Clerk's Department and the Supplementary Clerk then serving in the Consular Department were appointed to the two first class clerkships and were designated respectively 'Auditor and Examiner' and 'Bookkeeper and Accountant'.[9] The appointment of an additional Third Class Supplementary Clerk was authorised in 1869.[10]

One or occasionally two Extra Clerks were employed in the years 1825–65.[11] The Clerks of the Passport Office, created in 1855 and placed under the superintendence of the Chief Clerk, have not been included in these lists.

[1] FO 366/1292, payment 10 Oct. 1814.
[2] FO 366/672 p. 213.
[3] Order in council 28 March 1822 (PC 2/204 p. 86).
[4] FO 366/672 pp. 329–30.
[5] FO 366/673 p. 36.
[6] FO 366/674 p. 407.
[7] Order in council 3 July 1854 (FO 366/542 ff. 90–8).
[8] FO 366/675 pp. 543–50; FO 366/676 pp. 5–9, 104.
[9] FO 366/676 pp. 270–1, 395–404.
[10] FO 366/677 pp. 31–50.
[11] FO 366/1292, payment 22 July 1826; FO 366/673 p. 32; FO 366/674 pp. 549–53; FO 366/675 pp. 142–4.

CLERKS

1814	5 July	Scott, H. D.	1868	1 April	Plasket, E.
1854	1 July	Ayers, J.	1868	1 April	Foster, A.
1854	11 July	Grey, T. B.	1868	25 May	McCarthy, D.
1865	17 April	Newman, E. B.	1868	9 Sept.	Hertslet, E. C.
1867	23 Jan.	Woodgate, A. G. K.	1869	18 Aug.	Taylor, A. C.

EXTRA CLERKS

1826	17 April	Sanders, H. W.	1852	9 Feb.	Ayers, J.
1827	6 Jan.	Francklin, G. F.	1859	20 June	Newman, E. B.

Clerks attached to Treaty Department 1817–70

From 1817 J. B. Bergne was employed on a regular basis but without salary as a Clerk attached to the Treaty Department. In 1824 when a lithographic press was installed in the Foreign Office Bergne, who was authorised to prepare all handwritten material for it, was awarded an annual allowance of £150 from the contingent fund. In 1827 he was provided with a salary of £150 rising by annual increments of £10 to £300. The salary was increased in 1829 to £350 rising by annual increments of £15 to £545.[1] In 1841 the payment of the salary was transferred from the contingent fund to the fee fund.[2] An additional personal allowance of £100 was made available to Bergne in 1845.[3] In the years 1846–9 a second Clerk with a salary of £100 was attached to the Department.[4] In 1852 Bury, a Clerk who had been employed without salary in various of the subordinate departments since 1844, was attached exclusively to the Treaty Department.[5] On Bergne's appointment to the office of Superintendent of the Treaty Department in 1854, Bury was appointed his Clerk, or Assistant, at a salary of £200 rising by annual increments of £20 to £500.[6] In 1860 a second Clerk at a salary of £100 rising by annual increments of £10 to £250 was added to the Department.[7] In 1865 the two Clerks were allocated to the new grade of Supplementary Clerk: the First Clerk to the First Class at a salary of £400 rising by annual increments of £15 to £500, and the Second Clerk to the Second Class at a salary of £250 rising by annual increments of £15 to £360.[8]

1817	5 Jan.	Bergne, J. B.
1846	29 June	Bode, —
1846	17 Oct.	Wolff, H. D.
1852	12 Nov.	Bury, R.
1860	19 Nov.	March, G. E.

[1] FO 366/672 pp. 359, 366; FO 366/673 pp. 39–40, 99.
[2] Order in council 21 Aug. 1841 (FO 366/542 ff. 75–80).
[3] FO 366/674 p. 410.
[4] ibid. pp. 438, 445, 475–6.
[5] FO 366/449 p. 59.
[6] Order in council 3 July 1854 (FO 366/542 ff. 90–8).
[7] FO 366/675 pp. 259–64.
[8] ibid. pp. 543–50; FO 366/676 pp. 5–9.

Clerks attached to Slave Trade Department 1825–56

Until 1853 the Slave Trade Department was staffed by Clerks distinct from the regular clerical establishment. From 1825 to 1841 the salaries of the Clerks, usually three in number, were paid from the funds voted annually by Parliament to meet the expenses of various commissions for the suppression of the slave trade.[1] In 1841 it was provided that the salaries of four Clerks should be met from the fee fund. The salary of the First Clerk was fixed at £150 rising by annual increments of £10 to £300, of the Second Clerk at £100 rising by annual increments of £10 to £300 and of the Third and Fourth Clerks at £80 rising by annual increments of £10 to £150.[2] In 1844 Parnther, the First Clerk, was awarded an additional personal allowance of £100, payable out of the contingent fund.[3] An application made by the Foreign Office to the Treasury in 1848 for an increase in the salaries of the First and Second Clerks, Parnther and Scott, was not approved until 1853.[4] It was then provided that the salary of the First Clerk should be fixed at £350 rising by annual increments of £15 to £545. The increase took effect from 1850, and the allowance of £100 awarded in 1844 was assimilated to Parnther's salary. Scott's salary was fixed at the same level with effect from 1852. Parnther and Scott were dismissed in September 1853, for fraudulent use of money lodged in their hands as agents to slave trade commissioners serving abroad, and the opportunity was taken to reorganise the Department. Their places were temporarily supplied by established Clerks, until it was determined in 1854 that the Department should regularly be staffed by such Clerks.[5]

1825	22 Nov.	Pettingal, C.
1826	5 Dec.	Frere, G.
1827	19 April	Le Mesurier, J. J.
1834	16 June	Browne, J. H. T. T.
1835	27 April	Parnther, C. H.
1837	26 Jan.	Johnson, W.
1838	14 March	Browne, J. H. T. T.[6]
1840	5 Feb.	Parnther, C. H.[6]
1841	20 Aug.	Dowling, D. M.
1842	5 Nov.	Scott, H. C.
1845	28 Feb.	Skelton, G.
1845	21 Nov.	Dashwood, W. J. P.
1852	1 April	Dashwood, J. E. B.
1852	18 Oct.	Anderson, H. P.

[1] Information as to the salaries of individual Clerks, which ranged between £80 and £230, can be found in a collection of draft estimates of these expenses (FO 96/34).

[2] Order in council 21 Aug. 1841 (FO 366/542 ff. 75–80).

[3] FO 366/674 p. 374.

[4] ibid. pp. 464a–469; FO 366/449 pp. 75–8.

[5] FO 366/449 pp. 85–105; order in council 3 July 1854 (FO 366/542 ff. 90–8). Skelton remained exclusively attached to the Slave Trade Department, at a salary of £350 rising by annual increments of £15 to £545, until he left the Foreign Office in 1856.

[6] Reappointed.

Clerks attached to Librarian's Department 1826–70

A Temporary Clerk, or Assistant, was employed in the Librarian's Department in the years 1826–39. His salary, payable out of the contingent fund, was fixed at £100 in 1826 and increased to £150 in 1838.[1] In 1841 provision was made for two permanent Clerks to serve in the Department, the First with a salary of £100 rising by annual increments of £10 and £15 to £300, and the Second with a salary of £80 rising by annual increments of £10 and £15 to £250.[2] From 1841 to 1854 three or four Temporary Clerks were attached to the Department with salaries of £100 rising by annual increments of £10 to £150.[3] In 1854 the appointments of the three Temporary Clerks then in employment were made permanent. The salary of the First Clerk was fixed at £260 rising by annual increments of £15 to £350, of the Second at £200 rising by annual increments of £15 to £260, of the Third at £150 rising by annual increments of £10 to £200, and of the Fourth and Fifth at £100 rising by annual increments of £10 to £150.[4] A Temporary Clerk with a salary of £200 was again employed from 1862.[5] In 1865 the First to Third Clerks were placed in the new grade of Second Class Supplementary Clerk with salaries of £250 rising by annual increments of £15 to £360; the Fourth and Fifth Clerks were graded as Third Class Supplementary Clerks with salaries of £100 rising by annual increments of £10 to £240.[6] In 1868 arrears in registration and increased library accommodation in the new Foreign Office building necessitated the appointment of two additional Third Class Supplementary Clerks and five Temporary Clerks with salaries of £140.[7]

CLERKS

1841	24 Aug.	Seale, R. B.
1841	24 Aug.	Quick, W. F.
1844	28 Aug.	Hertslet, E.
1844	10 Nov.	Sasse, F. R.
1854	1 July	Green, A. S.
1854	1 July	Irving, F.
1854	1 July	Walmisley, A.
1855	25 April	March, G. E.
1858	5 April	Oakes, A. H.
1859	17 Jan.	Sasse, F. R.[8]
1861	29 Jan.	Robertson, D.
1868	12 May	Bagot, E. A. J.
1868	22 Dec.	Streatfield, F. H. T.

[1] FO 366/673 pp. 4, 401.

[2] Order in council 21 Aug. 1841 (FO 366/542 ff. 75–80).

[3] FO 366/674 pp. 36–9.

[4] Order in council 3 July 1854 (FO 366/542 ff. 90–8). The salaries of the Third and Fourth Clerks were increased in 1855 to the levels awarded in 1854 to the Second and Third Clerks respectively (FO 366/449 pp. 397–401).

[5] FO 366/675 p. 406.

[6] ibid. pp. 543–50; FO 366/676 pp. 5–9.

[7] FO 366/676 pp. 211–29.

[8] Reappointed.

TEMPORARY CLERKS

1826	5 April	Wilson, R.	1845	9 Aug.	Walmisley, A.
1841	24 Aug.	Lumley, J. S.	1862	29 Jan.	Carpenter, P.
1841	24 Aug.	Mann, H.	1868	1 July	Frere, G.
1841	24 Aug.	Rich, H. O. L.	1868	1 July	Neale, H. St. J.
1842	8 Jan.	Hertslet, E.	1868	1 July	Romer, A.
1844	28 Nov.	Taunton, W. G.	1868	1 July	Barnett, H. B.
1844	19 Dec.	Green, A. S.	1869	15 April	Fraser, H. W.
1845	7 May	Irving, F.	1870	20 May	Hertslet, R. H.

Clerk attached to Consular Department 1826–68

The business of the Consular Department was normally conducted by established Clerks. In the years 1826–39, however, a Supplementary Clerk was attached to the Department. The salary, payable out of the contingent fund, was fixed at £100 in 1826, increased to £125 in 1830 and to £150 in 1834, and again reduced to £100 in 1835. In 1839 provision was made for the Clerk's salary to increase by annual increments of £10 to £150.[1] In 1860 an official described as a 'Supplemental Junior Clerk' was attached to the Department to keep the consular accounts at a salary of £150 rising by annual increments of £15 to £300.[2] The Clerk was placed in the new grade of Second Class Supplementary Clerk in 1865 with a salary of £250 rising by annual increments of £15 to £360.[3] The office was discontinued in 1868 when the duty of keeping the consular accounts was transferred to the Chief Clerk's Department.

1826	5 July	Saunders, S. S.
1835	18 April	Francklin, G. F.
1860	16 Nov.	Gladwell, W.
1861	30 Aug.	Plasket, E.

[1] FO 366/673 pp. 19, 154, 229, 279, 400.

[2] FO 366/675 pp. 259–64. Gladwell, the first holder of the office, who was transferred from the Admiralty (Accountants Branch), was granted a salary of £215 on his appointment (ibid. pp. 286–8). The minimum was increased to £200 in 1863 (ibid. pp. 449–50).

[3] ibid. pp. 543–50; FO 366/676 pp. 5–9.

Librarian and Keeper of the Papers and Sub-Librarian 1801–70

The office of Librarian and Keeper of the Papers was created in 1801 following the reorganisation of the State Paper Office.[1] The salary, payable out of the contingent fund, was fixed at £200 in 1801 and increased to £300 in 1815.[2] In 1811 the office was brought within the terms of the order in council of May 1809 which provided increases in salary of £80, £200, £300 and £400 after successive periods of five years' service.[3] In 1822 the office was placed on the establishment with a salary of £350 rising by annual increments of £15 to £545. However, L. Hertslet, the Librarian in office in 1822, was already receiving a salary of £700 by virtue of his having completed twenty years' service in the Foreign Office, and this salary he was allowed to retain.[4] Until 1837 Hertslet received an annual allowance of £100 from the secret service fund for compiling from the newspapers volumes of 'Printed Public Documents'. From 1837 this allowance was paid from the fee fund as part of his regular salary, which was thus increased to £800.[5] In 1841 the salary of the Librarian was fixed at £600 rising by annual increments of £20 to £800.[6]

A Sub-Librarian served without salary from 1801. A salary of £50, payable out of the contingent fund, was first made available to the holder of the office in 1809.[7] The salary was increased to £100 in 1813.[8] In 1816 the office was brought within the terms of the order in council of May 1809 which provided increases in salary of £80, £200, £300 and £400 after successive periods of five years' service.[9] In 1822 it was placed on the establishment with a salary of £150 rising by annual increments of £10 to £350. The duties of the office of 'Entering and Dispatch Clerk', formerly performed by an Extra Clerk, were also transferred to the Sub-Librarian who was accordingly awarded an additional annual allowance of £100.[10] In 1827 the salary was increased to £350 rising by annual increments of £15 to £545.[11] In 1865 it was provided that future holders of the office should be graded as First Class Supplementary Clerks with a salary of £400 rising by annual increments of £15 to £500.[12]

[1] FO 366/672 pp. 2–4. Ancell, the first holder, had served in the State Paper Office from Nov. 1776.

[2] FO 366/1292, payment 10 Feb. 1802; FO 366/672 pp. 98, 102.

[3] FO 366/672 pp. 30–1.

[4] Order in council 28 March 1822 (PC 2/204 p. 86); FO 366/381–2.

[5] FO 366/673 p. 333. From 1825 Hertslet also received irregular payments from the secret service fund as compiler of *British and Foreign State Papers* (FO 366/674 pp. 273–82). In addition he served 1824–54 as Superintendent of King's Messengers, an office which lies outside the scope of this volume.

[6] Order in council 21 Aug. 1841 (FO 366/542 ff. 75–80).

[7] FO 366/671 p. 396.

[8] FO 366/672 pp. 62–3.

[9] ibid. pp. 111, 113.

[10] Order in council 28 March 1822 (PC 2/204 p. 86). Although the duties of 'Entering and Dispatch Clerk' were assumed by a Clerk on the establishment in 1842, J. Hertslet continued to receive the allowance until his retirement in 1855 (FO 366/674 pp. 153–5).

[11] FO 366/673 p. 37.

[12] FO 366/675 pp. 543–50; FO 366/676 pp. 5–9.

LIBRARIAN AND KEEPER OF THE PAPERS

1801	5 Jan.	Ancell, R.
1810	6 Jan.	Hertslet, L.
1857	19 Nov.	Hertslet, E.

SUB-LIBRARIAN

1801	5 Feb.	Hertslet, L.
1811	29 March	Hertslet, J.
1855	1 April	Hertslet, E.
1857	3 Dec.	Sasse, F. R.[13]
1859	17 Jan.	Green, A. S.

[13] Probationary.

Translator and Assistant Translator 1809–70

A salary of £300 was made available in 1809 to a Translator of the Spanish, Portuguese, Italian and Danish Languages.[1] In 1814 the official, who soon became known simply as the Translator, was brought within the terms of the order in council of May 1809 which provided increases in salary of £80, £200, £300 and £400 after successive periods of five years' service.[2] The salary was again fixed at £300 in 1822.[3] It was increased to £500 in 1854.[4]

A salary of £200, payable out of the contingent fund, was made available to an Assistant Translator in 1823.[5] In 1827 provision was made for the salary to increase by annual increments of £15 to a maximum of £300.[6] The office was abolished in 1831.[7]

TRANSLATOR

1809	11 Jan.	Huttner, J. C.
1847	28 Nov.	Norris, E.
1866	1 April	Cannon, C.

ASSISTANT TRANSLATOR

1823	27 Oct.	Masterton, C.

[1] Order in council 11 Jan. 1809 (FO 366/671 pp. 362–3). For the sinecure office of Translator of the German Language attached to the Foreign Office in 1782, abolished in 1802 and revived 1806–9, see *Officials of the Secretaries of State*, 49.

[2] FO 366/672 p. 67.

[3] Order in council 28 March 1822 (PC 2/204 p. 86). Huttner, the Translator in office in 1822, continued to receive an increment of £265 in respect of his 14 years' service prior to 1822, until his death in 1847.

[4] Order in council 3 July 1854 (FO 366/542 ff. 90–8).

[5] FO 366/672 p. 338.

[6] FO 366/673 p. 38.

[7] ibid. pp. 167, 173.

Precis Writers 1793–1870

The office of Précis Writer, or Secretary of the Précis as it was originally designated, first acquired official standing in 1793 when a salary of £300, payable out of the contingent fund, was made available to its holder.[1] The office was placed on the establishment in 1795.[2] Until 1852 the office was usually held by relations or personal friends of the Secretary of State, who entered and left office with him; many of them subsequently held office in the diplomatic service.[3] After the appointment of Bridges Taylor in 1852 the office was invariably held by Clerks on the establishment. No salary was paid to Précis Writers who were members of the House of Commons.[4] In the years 1829 to 1831 one third of the salary was made available to Dawkins, who was designated Acting Précis Writer. W. J. Hamilton drew two thirds of the salary from April to November 1830. Temple who held the office 1830–2 drew no salary, probably because he was already in receipt of a salary as Secretary of Embassy, St. Petersburg.[5]

From January to April 1805 a salary of £80, payable out of the contingent fund, was made available to an Assistant Précis Writer.[6] In the months July to October 1807 Planta, a Clerk on the establishment, drew one third of the salary of the main office as Assistant Précis Writer while S. Canning, the Précis Writer, drew two thirds.[7] A similar private arrangement may have been made between Canning and his Assistant, Douglas, from November 1807 to January 1809. In the years 1814 to 1819 a Clerk on the establishment received an allowance of £100, payable out of the contingent fund, as Assistant Précis Writer.[8] Several other individuals are mentioned in the *Foreign Office Lists* as having held the office of Assistant Précis Writer for short periods.[9] They have not been included in this list as they appear to have had no formal status in the Foreign Office establishment.

1793	29 Sept.	Arbuthnot, C.
1795	5 April	Wesley, Hon. H.
1797	10 Oct.	Bruce, Hon. J.
1798	5 Sept.	Taylor, B.

[1] FO 366/1292, payment 3 Nov. 1794.

[2] Order in council 27 Feb. 1795 (*16th Rept. on Finance*, 309–11).

[3] Before 1852 only Planta (1809–17), Sulivan (1832–3), Stopford (1841–3) and Paget (1846) held the office while serving as Clerks. Sulivan received no salary as a Clerk while holding the office (FO 366/673 p. 218). Brook Taylor (1798–1801) and Planta (1814–17) held the office jointly with that of Private Secretary to the Secretary of State and drew the full salary attached to both offices.

[4] FO 366/383, case of Anson, whose salary ceased 5 July 1847 on his election. H. E. J. Stanley, who was designated Assistant Précis Writer, drew the full salary of £300 from 20 Dec. 1847 until he succeeded Anson *c.* April 1849 (FO 366/674 p. 461). Arbuthnot (1795) and Gordon Lennox (1846) left office on being elected members of the House of Commons; Bruce (1797) resigned his seat so that he could draw the salary of the office (FO 366/671 p. 45).

[5] FO 366/673 pp. 101, 138, 159, 165.

[6] FO 366/1292, payment 15 Aug. 1805.

[7] FO 366/380.

[8] FO 366/672 pp. 88, 176.

[9] See *FOL* (March 1868), 6 for the fullest list.

1801	20 Feb.	Williams Wynn, H. W.
1803	5 April	Jenkinson, Hon. C. C. C.
1804	5 April	Hamilton, W. R.
1805	5 Jan.	Woodcock, C. (*Assistant*)
1806	6 March	Trotter, J. B.
1807	5 July	Canning, S.
1807	5 July	Planta, J. (*Assistant*)
1807	Nov.	Douglas, A. S. (*Assistant*)
1809	5 Jan.	Planta, J.
1814	1 Jan.	Graham, D. (*Assistant*)
1817	5 Jan.	Lenox Conyngham, G. (*Assistant*)
1817	5 July	Cartwright, T.
1821	5 Jan.	Seymour, G. H.
1822	29 Jan.	Hill, Lord A. M. C.
1822	10 Oct.	Howard de Walden, Lord
1824	5 July	Dunglas, Lord
1827	5 July	Abercromby, R.
1828	12 Aug.	Ashburnham, Hon. C.
1829	27 Aug.	Dawkins, C. G. A. (*Acting*)
1830	5 April	Hamilton, W. J.
1830	22 Nov.	Temple, Hon. W.
1832	16 Sept.	Sulivan, S. H.

1833	3 May	Ponsonby, J. G. B.
1834	17 Nov.	Greville, H. W.
1835	27 April	Howard, Hon. J. K.
1840	5 Jan.	Pleydell Bouverie, Hon. E.
1840	20 April	Elliot, Hon. H. G.
1841	3 Sept.	Stopford, W. B.
1843	25 Nov.	Hamilton Gordon, Hon. A.
1845	18 Feb.	Gordon Lennox, Lord H. G. C.
1846	5 Feb.	Paget, A. B.
1846	9 July	Anson, Viscount
1847	20 Dec.	Stanley, H. E. J. (*Assistant*)
1849	*c.* April	Stanley, Hon. H. E. J.
1851	30 Dec.	Leveson Gower, Hon. E. F.
1852	27 Feb.	Hamond, H.
1852	1 April	Taylor, B.
1852	14 Dec.	Bidwell, J.
1852	29 Dec.	Cavendish, F. W. H.
1857	9 Dec.	Currie, P. H. W.
1858	26 Feb.	Dashwood, J. E. B.
1859	18 June	Lister, T. V.
1865	3 Nov.	Hervey, H. A. W.
1866	6 July	Abbott, C. S. A.
1868	10 Dec.	Hervey, H. A. W.

Private Secretaries to Secretary of State 1795–1870

The office of Private Secretary to the Secretary of State first acquired official standing in 1795 when a salary of £300 was made available to its holder.[1] Before 1824 only Planta held the office while serving as a Clerk on the establishment. Thereafter Clerks frequently held the office.[2]

At various times an Assistant Private Secretary held office, usually without salary. In the years 1808–9 and 1826–7 a salary of £150, payable out of the contingent fund, was made available to the Assistant Private Secretary.[3]

Grenville	1791–1801	1795	5 Jan.	Goddard, C.
		1796	24 Feb.	Taylor, B.
		1801	1 Feb.	Williams Wynn, H. W.
Hawkesbury	1801–4	1801	20 Feb.	Lamb, T. D.
		1802	5 July	Pierrepont, Hon. H. M.
Harrowby	1804–5	1804	*c.* May	Hamilton, W. R.
		1804	5 July	Woodcock, C.
Mulgrave	1805–6	1805	Jan.	Smith, G.
Fox	1806	1806	7 Feb.	Trotter, J. B.
Howick	1806–7	1806	24 Sept.	Trotter, J. B.
		1806	12 Dec.	Talbot, R.
Canning	1807–9	1807	5 April	Ross, J. T.
		1808	10 Oct.	Turner, W. (*Assistant*)
Bathurst	1809	1809	11 Oct.	Vaughan, C. R.
Wellesley	1809–12	1810	5 Jan.	Forbes, J.
Castlereagh/ Londonderry	1812–22	1812	10 Oct.	Ward, E. M.
		1814	5 July	Planta, J.
		1817	5 July	Clanwilliam, Earl of
		1819	5 July	Ancram, Earl of
		1820	5 Jan.	Clanwilliam, Earl of
		1822	29 Jan.	Seymour, G. H.
Canning	1822–7	1822	10 Oct.	Cavendish Bentinck, Lord W. G. F.

[1] Order in council 27 Feb. 1795 (*16th Rept. on Finance*, 309–11).

[2] Brook Taylor (1796–1801) and Williams Wynn (1801) were Clerks when appointed to the office of Private Secretary. Both ceased to draw salary as Clerks on their appointment, but were allowed to retain their rank in the clerical establishment should they wish subsequently to return to their duties (FO 366/670 p. 371; FO 366/671 p. 155). Neither, in fact, resumed his clerkship. Thereafter, of the Clerks appointed to the office only Sulivan (1833–4) was not permitted to draw his salary as a Clerk (FO 366/673 p. 218; FO 366/382).

[3] FO 366/671 p. 356; FO 366/673 p. 30.

		1824	5 April	Stapleton, A. G.
		1826	1 Nov.	Liddell, Hon. T. (*Assistant*)
Dudley	1827–8	1827	30 April	Wrangham, D. C.
		1827	30 April	Liddell, Hon. T. (*Assistant*)
Aberdeen	1828–30	1828	30 May	Wrangham, D. C.
Palmerston	1830–4	1830	25 Nov.	Walpole, Hon. J.
		1833	3 May	Sulivan, S. H.
Wellington	1834–5	1834	17 Nov.	Greville, A. F.
Palmerston	1835–41	1835	11 May	Cowper, Hon. C. S.
		1840	5 Jan.	Howard, Hon. J. K.
Aberdeen	1841–6	1841	3 Sept.	Dawkins, C. G. A.
		1841	3 Sept.	Hamilton Gordon, Hon. A. (*Assistant*)
Palmerston	1846–51	1846	9 July	Ponsonby, Hon. S. C. B.
Granville	1851–2	1851	26 Dec.	Ponsonby, Hon. S. C. B.
Malmesbury	1852	1852	27 Feb.	Harris, G.
Russell	1852–3	1852	29 Dec.	Russell, A. J. E.
		1852	29 Dec.	Boileau, J. E. (*Assistant*)
Clarendon	1853–8	1853	22 Feb.	Ponsonby, Hon. S. C. B.
		1853	22 Feb.	Lister, T. V. (*Assistant*)
		1855	12 Feb.	Fullerton, W. G. (*Assistant*)
		1857	7 Dec.	Lister, T. V.
Malmesbury	1858–9	1858	26 Feb.	Bidwell, J.
		1858	26 Feb.	Wolff, H. D. (*Assistant*)
Russell	1859–65	1859	18 June	Elliot, Hon. G. F. S.
		1859	19 June	Russell, G. (*Assistant*)
Clarendon	1865–6	1865	3 Nov.	Lister, T. V.
Stanley	1866–8	1866	6 July	Sanderson, T. H.
Clarendon	1868–70	1868	10 Dec.	Lister, T. V.
Granville	1870	1870	6 July	Meade, Hon. R. H.

Assistant to Under Secretaries 1801–26

In 1801 an annual allowance of £250 was made available to S. Rolleston, the First Senior Clerk, who for 'a considerable time past' had been employed as Assistant to the Under Secretaries.[1] Rolleston continued to receive the allowance while serving both as Second Chief Clerk and Chief Clerk until his retirement in 1824, when it was made available to the First Senior Clerk, J. Bidwell. The allowance was discontinued in 1826 when Bidwell was appointed Superintendent of the newly formed Consular Department.[2]

1801	20 Feb.	Rolleston, S.
1824	2 Feb.	Bidwell, J.

[1] Order in council 16 June 1801 (FO 366/671 pp. 186–8).
[2] FO 366/672 pp. 429–32.

Clerks Assistant to Under Secretaries 1822–41

On the reorganisation of the Foreign Office in 1822 annual allowances of £150 were made available to the two most junior Clerks on the establishment as 'Private Secretaries to the Under Secretaries'.[1] In 1831 Palmerston directed that, as their duties were of a public and not a private nature, they should henceforth be designated Clerks Assistant to the Under Secretaries.[2] The latter term has been used throughout these lists. The number of Clerks Assistant was increased to three in 1824 and to four in 1836.[3] After 1822 receipt of the allowance was not restricted to Junior Clerks. From 1824 until 1839 all Clerks Assistant were Second Class Clerks, who became effectively superintendents of the work in the Political Departments of the office. On his promotion to a senior clerkship in 1834, Lenox Conyngham surrendered both the allowance and the duties of a Clerk Assistant. On Staveley's promotion to a senior clerkship in 1839, however, he retained both his allowance and his duties. In 1841 the three other Clerks Assistant were promoted to the enlarged senior grade and became in name as well as in fact Superintendents of the Political Departments. It was then provided that the four Clerks Assistant should retain their allowances of £150 until their retirement, but that their maximum salaries as Senior Clerks should be restricted to £850 rather than £1,000.[4]

1822	28 March	Staveley, T.
1822	28 March	Parish, W.
1823	10 Oct.	Bankhead, C.
1824	5 July	Lenox Conyngham, G.
1825	5 Jan.	Ward, T. L.
1831	5 July	Mellish, R. C.
1834	5 July	Ward, T. L.[5]
1836	26 April	Hammond, E.

[1] Order in council 28 March 1822 (PC 2/204 p. 86). The two Clerks awarded the allowance in 1822 had probably performed the duties of the office before that date. Staveley had been awarded an allowance of one guinea a day, payable out of the contingent fund, during the absence of the Under Secretary, W. R. Hamilton, 14 April 1820–30 July 1821 (FO 366/1292, payments 27 July 1820, 20 Aug. 1821; FO 366/672 pp. 186, 212). Parish had been awarded an annual allowance of £150, payable out of the contingent fund, in 1820 for extra duties on confidential business (FO 366/672 pp. 205, 209).

[2] FO 366/673 p. 162.

[3] FO 366/672 p. 394; FO 366/673 p. 314.

[4] Order in council 21 Aug. 1841 (FO 366/542 ff. 75–80); FO 366/674 pp. 5–12.

[5] Reappointed.

Private Secretary to Parliamentary Under Secretary 1866–70

In 1866 the Parliamentary Under Secretary was authorised to appoint a Private Secretary, selected from the Junior Clerks on the establishment, with an additional allowance of £150.[1]

Layard	1866	1866	1 Feb.	Sanderson, T. H.
Egerton	1866–8	1866	6 July	Clarke Jervoise, H. S. C.
Otway	1868	1868	12 Dec.	Barrington, Hon. B. E. E.

[1] FO 366/676 pp. 92–3, 95.

Superintendent of Treaty Department 1813–70

In 1813 H. J. Rolleston, a Clerk on the establishment, was awarded an annual allowance of £150 for engrossing treaties with foreign powers, diplomatic commissions and other instruments to be signed by the monarch or to pass the great seal.[1] On his promotion to a senior clerkship in 1824 Rolleston continued to receive the allowance and thereafter was usually known as Superintendent of the Treaty Department. Lenox Conyngham, who succeeded to Rolleston's senior clerkship in 1834, also received the allowance until his promotion to the chief clerkship in 1841 when the superintendence of the Treaty Department became a function of the Chief Clerk.[2] In 1854 the Treaty Department was removed from the control of the Chief Clerk and placed under a Superintendent with a salary of £600 rising by annual increments of £25 to £800.[3] In 1862 an additional personal allowance of £200 was made available to the then Superintendent, J. B. Bergne.[4]

1813	5 April	Rolleston, H. J.
1834	5 July	Lenox Conyngham, G.
1854	1 July	Bergne, J. B.

[1] FO 366/672 pp. 68–70.
[2] FO 366/673 pp. 261–3; FO 366/674 pp. 5–12.
[3] Order in council 3 July 1854 (FO 366/542 ff. 90–8).
[4] FO 366/675 pp. 420–1, 423–4.

Superintendent of Slave Trade Department 1824–45

In 1824 an annual allowance of £200, payable from the funds voted annually by Parliament to meet the expenses of various commissions for the suppression of the slave trade, was awarded to Bandinel, the Second Senior Clerk, as Superintendent of the Slave Trade Department.[1] The allowance had been increased to £400 by 1828.[2] In 1841 it was provided that the allowance should be discontinued on Bandinel's retirement, which took place in 1845.[3] Thereafter the duty was performed without any additional allowance by one of the Senior Clerks.

1824	5 Jan.	Bandinel, J.

[1] FO 83/40, 4 Dec. 1824. At the same time Bandinel was awarded a sum of £1,000, payable out of monies arising from the sale of condemned slave vessels, for his services in the previous five years.
[2] FO 96/28/1 ff. 3–4.
[3] FO 366/674 pp. 5–12.

Superintendent of Consular Department 1826–51

In 1826 an annual allowance of £500 was made available to J. Bidwell, the First Senior Clerk, as Superintendent of the newly formed Consular Department.[1] In 1841 it was provided that the allowance should be discontinued on Bidwell's retirement, which took place in 1851.[2] Thereafter the duty was performed without any additional allowance by one of the Senior Clerks.

1826	5 Jan.	Bidwell, J.

[1] FO 366/672 pp. 429–32.
[2] FO 366/674 pp. 5–12.

Superintendent of Foreign Ministers' Accounts 1827–39

In 1827 Byng, the only Senior Clerk not receiving an allowance for the performance of a specific area of duty, was awarded an annual allowance of £150 to examine the contingent accounts of diplomats and consuls.[1] Thereafter he was usually designated Superintendent of Foreign Ministers' Accounts. On Byng's retirement in 1839, the duty was transferred to the Chief Clerk.[2]

1827	5 Jan.	Byng, Hon. F. G.

[1] FO 366/673 pp. 28–9, 44–5.
[2] ibid. pp. 376–7.

Superintendent of Commercial and Consular Department 1866–70

On the formation of the Commercial and Consular Department in 1866, an annual allowance of £250 was made available to the Senior Clerk selected to superintend its work.[1]

1866	1 Oct.	Spring Rice, Hon. T. C. W.
1869	3 July	Wylde, W. H.

[1] FO 366/676 pp. 122–4, 136–7.

Office Keepers 1782–1870

Two Office, or Chamber, Keepers, one of whom acted by Deputy, were taken over by the Foreign Office from the former Northern Department. In 1824 a Third, or Assistant, Office Keeper was appointed, and in 1853 a Fourth.[1] The salaries of the Third and Fourth Office Keepers were paid from the contingent fund until both offices were placed on the establishment in 1854.[2] The number of Office Keepers was increased to five in 1861 and to seven in 1868.[3]

Until 1795 the two Office Keepers received salaries of £20 16s. each from the Secretary of State together with office fees and certain other perquisites.[4] In 1795 the salaries were fixed at £100 each.[5] In 1845 the salary of the First Office Keeper was increased to £200 in lieu of all perquisites and emoluments.[6] The salary of the Third Office Keeper was fixed at £100 in 1824 and increased to £150 in lieu of all perquisites and emoluments in 1843.[7] The salary of the Fourth Office Keeper was fixed at £100 in 1853 and increased to £125 in 1856.[8] The salaries of the Fifth to Seventh Office Keepers were fixed at £125.[9]

1782	March	Turner, R.
1782	March	Schaw, J.
c. 1787		Ancell, T.[10]
c. 1790		Precious, W.
1795	5 April	Walpole, J.[11]
1795	10 Oct.	Bulgin, A.
1797	5 Jan.	Coral, F.
1807	22 Jan.	Conway, J.
1812	5 Jan.	Munton, A.
1812	26 Feb.	Burman, H.
1824	8 March	Aspain, H.
1824	24 Nov.	Reed, J.
1825	5 July	Venfield, J.
1826	5 April	Stahl, C.
1834	24 Sept.	Cocking, H. V.
1838	3 March	Samways, J.
1838	2 Aug.	Tyler, J.
1843	2 Oct.	Coxhead, G.
1845	12 Dec.	Greenall, W.
1853	5 Sept.	Christopher, G.

[1] FO 366/672 pp. 379, 385; FO 366/449 p. 84.

[2] Order in council 3 July 1854 (FO 366/542 ff. 90–8).

[3] FO 366/675 pp. 374, 383; FO 366/676 pp. 353–9.

[4] *1st Rept. on Fees*, 7, 32–3.

[5] Order in council 27 Feb. 1795 (*16th Rept. on Finance*, 309–11). From January to October 1797 one of the salaries was shared by Bulgin and Walpole. On his retirement in 1807, Walpole continued to receive his full salary. His successor, Conway, was awarded an allowance of £25, increased to £50 later in 1807 and to £100 in 1811, payable out of the contingent fund. On Conway's death in 1812, Walpole was awarded a retirement allowance of £100 (FO 366/671 pp. 314, 340–1; FO 366/672 pp. 18–19; FO 366/380).

[6] FO 366/674 p. 402.

[7] FO 366/672 pp. 379, 385; FO 366/674 p. 264. From 1862 the salary of £150 was paid to the Second Office Keeper and that of the Third Office Keeper fell to £125 (FO 366/384).

[8] FO 366/449 pp. 84, 420.

[9] FO 366/675 pp. 374, 383; FO 366/676 pp. 353–9.

[10] Served as Deputy Office Keeper from March 1782.

[11] Served as Assistant Office Keeper with a salary of £100 from 1 Aug. 1793.

1857	31 Jan.	Rolfe, R.	1868	11 March	Catchpole, G.
1861	21 Oct.	Haley, J.	1868	21 Aug.	Batterbee, T. O.
1862	17 Jan.	Johnson, H.	1868	21 Aug.	Hansen, C. R. B.
1863	31 July	Dalbertanson, C. I.	1869	24 Aug.	Pearl, A. C.
1864	20 July	Vincent, G.			

Housekeeper 1782–1870

The office of Housekeeper, or Necessary Woman as it was originally designated, was taken over by the Foreign Office from the former Northern Department. Until 1795 the Housekeeper received a salary of £48 from the Secretary of State together with certain perquisites.[1] In 1795 the salary was fixed at £100.[2] In 1869 an additional annual allowance of £25 was provided as the Housekeeper was required to provide and serve luncheons for the staff employed in the new Foreign Office building.[3]

1782	March	Southcott, M.	1814	18 May	Trench, J.
1783		Cheese, A.	1824	5 July	Urquhart, M.
1805	5 Jan.	Mallet, A. J.	1836	18 March	Watson, A.
1806	5 July	Dassonville, M.	1863	26 Nov.	Langcake, M.

[1] *1st Rept. on Fees*, 7, 33.
[2] Order in council 27 Feb. 1795 (*16th Rept. on Finance*, 309–11).
[3] FO 366/676 pp. 482–8.

Office Porters c. 1785–1870

An Office Porter or Messenger was in employment by 1784 and the succession to the office can be established from 1791.[1] The office was frequently executed by one or two Deputies before 1843.[2] At first the Office Porter received no salary but was paid separate sums for each task that he performed and enjoyed the use of apartments in the Foreign Office.[3] On the death of the then Office Porter, Talbot, in 1843 provision was made for salaries of £230 and £120 to be paid out of the contingent fund to a Head Office Porter and a Second Office Porter or Under Porter.[4] The offices were placed on the establishment in 1854.[5]

OFFICE PORTER AND HEAD OFFICE PORTER

occ. 1785	Chaplin, T.	1795	July	Talbot, J.
by 1791	Cook, J.	1843	6 July	Catchpole, J.

SECOND OFFICE PORTER

1843	6 July	Spyer, E.
1851	26 July	Mills, T.

[1] *1st Rept. on Fees*, 8, 32; *Royal Kal.* (1791), 104.
[2] Four Deputies, Greenall, A. Spyer, E. Spyer and T. Talbot, have been identified.
[3] *1st Rept. on Fees*, 8, 32; FO 366/393, Sept. 1824.
[4] FO 366/674 pp. 239–44.
[5] Order in council 3 July 1854 (FO 366/542 ff. 90–8).

Doorkeepers c. 1786–1870

The office of Doorkeeper, or Door Porter, was probably created in 1786.[1] The salary, payable out of the contingent fund, was £67 6s. in 1792. It was increased to £94 12s. in 1800.[2] The office was placed on the establishment in 1822.[3] The salary was increased to £100 in 1841.[4]

In 1826 a salary of £50, payable out of the contingent fund, was made available to an Assistant, or Extra, Doorkeeper.[5] The office was placed on the establishment in 1854.[6] The salary was increased to £80 in 1841 and to £100 in 1860.[7]

DOORKEEPER

c. 1786		Dakin, W.	1815	5 July	Gracewood, A.
1810	10 Oct.	Burman, H.	1851	10 Feb.	Weller, J.
1812	26 Feb.	Graham, A.			

ASSISTANT DOORKEEPER

1826	5 Jan.	Addison, R.	1855	1 Jan.	Haley, J.
1827	27 Aug.	Kettle, H.	1861	21 Oct.	Johnson, H.
1841	27 Dec.	Catchpole, J.	1862	15 March	Dalbertanson, C. I.
1843	6 July	Greenall, W.	1863	19 Aug.	Catchpole, G.
1845	12 Dec.	Forsyth, W.	1868	9 April	Maynard, R. J.
1849	9 Oct.	Maulden, G.			

[1] It was not mentioned by the Commissioners on Fees, who reported 11 April 1786, and was listed for the first time in the *Royal Kalendar* in 1787.
[2] FO 366/1292, payments 11 July 1792, 5 April 1800.
[3] Order in council 28 March 1822 (PC 2/204 p. 86).
[4] Order in council 21 Aug. 1841 (FO 366/542 ff. 75–80).
[5] FO 366/672 p. 452.
[6] Order in council 3 July 1854 (FO 366/542 ff. 90–8).
[7] FO 366/674 p. 150: FO 366/675 pp. 239, 374, 402.

Printer 1800–70

In 1800 a salary of £150, payable out of the contingent fund, was made available to a Printer.[1] The office was placed on the establishment in 1822.[2]

1800	15 May	Harrison, J.
1847	23 March	Harrison, T. R.
1869	6 May	Harrison, T.

[1] FO 366/1292, payment 6 Nov. 1800.
[2] Order in council 28 March 1822 (PC 2/204 p. 86).

Lamplighter and Coal Porter c. 1806–70

Before 1806 an allowance was made available to the Housekeeper from the contingent fund for the purpose of employing a man servant to perform menial tasks. From 1806 a salary was paid directly to the servant who was subsequently designated Lamplighter and Coal Porter.[1] The office was placed on the establishment in 1854.[2] The salary, £67 6s. in 1806, was increased to £80 in 1813 and to £94 12s. in 1832.[3]

by 1806		Werry, J.	1840	7 July	Moore, T.
1812	10 Oct.	Garrod, J.	1852	15 Oct.	Farmer, T.
1817	6 May	Kingsbury, J.			

[1] FO 366/1292, payment 9 May 1806.
[2] Order in council 3 July 1854 (FO 366/542 ff. 90–8).
[3] FO 366/1292, payments 9 May 1806, 5 April 1813; FO 366/673 p. 211.

Messengers attached to Librarian's Department 1857–70

In 1857 a salary of £90 was made available to a Messenger attached exclusively to the Librarian's Department.[1] An allowance of one guinea a week was made available to a Second Messenger in 1869.[2]

1857	21 April	Mason, G.
1869	5 July	Hall, R. K.

[1] FO 366/449 p. 521.
[2] FO 366/676 p. 471.

Periodic Lists of Officials

LIST OF OFFICIALS ON THE FORMATION OF THE DEPARTMENT 27 MARCH 1782

Secretary of State
Fox, Hon. C. J.
Under Secretaries
Fraser, W.
Sheridan, R. B.
Chief Clerk
Sneyd, J.

Clerks
Broughton, B.
Aust, G.
Bidwell, T.
Carter, R.
Jenkins, J. W.
Money, W.
Manby, J.

Office Keepers
Turner, R.
Schaw, J.
Deputy Office Keeper
Ancell, T.
Housekeeper
Southcott, M.

LIST OF OFFICIALS ON CANNING'S LEAVING THE DEPARTMENT 30 APRIL 1827

Secretary of State
Canning, G.
Under Secretaries
Backhouse, J.
Howard de Walden, Lord
Clanricarde, Marquess of
Chief Clerk
Bidwell, T.
Senior Clerks
Bidwell, J.
Bandinel, J.
Byng, Hon. F. G.
Rolleston, H. J.
Second Class Clerks
Jackson, J.
Scheener, E.
Lenox Conyngham, G.
Staveley, T.
Ward, T. L.
McMahon, E.
Stapleton, A. G.

Junior Clerks
Mellish, R. C.
Mildmay, H. C. St. J.
Hammond, E.
Turner, A.
Oom, A. K.
Hervey, Lord W.
Assistant Junior Clerks
Lowth, G.
Stopford, W. B.
Adams, W. P.
Robinson, H. S.
Murray, J.
Ryder, Hon. F. D.
Edwardes, Hon. R.
Wrangham, D. C.
Clerks attached to Chief Clerk's Department
Scott, H. D.
Francklin, G. F. (*Extra*)
Sanders, H. W. (*Extra*)
Superintendent of Consular Department
Bidwell, J.

Clerk attached to Consular Department
Saunders, S. S.
Superintendent of Slave Trade Department
Bandinel, J.
Clerks attached to Slave Trade Department
Pettingal, C.
Frere, G.
Le Mesurier, J. J.
Superintendent of Treaty Department
Rolleston, H. J.
Clerk attached to Treaty Department
Bergne, J. B.
Superintendent of Foreign Ministers' Accounts
Byng, Hon. F. G.
Librarian
Hertslet, L.
Sub-Librarian
Hertslet, J.

Temporary Clerk attached to Librarian's Department
Wilson, R.
Translator
Huttner, J. C.
Assistant Translator
Masterton, C.
Précis Writer
Dunglas, Lord
Private Secretaries to Secretary of State
Stapleton, A. G.
Liddell, Hon. T. (*Assistant*)
Clerks Assistant to Under Secretaries
Staveley, T.
Lenox Conyngham, G.
Ward, T. L.
Office Keepers
Aspain, H.
Stahl, C.
Venfield, J.
Housekeeper
Urquhart, M.
Office Porter
Talbot, J.
Deputy Office Porter
Spyer, E.
Doorkeepers
Gracewood, A.
Addison, R.
Printer
Harrison, J.
Lamplighter and Coal Porter
Kingsbury, J.

LIST OF OFFICIALS FOLLOWING REORGANISATION 1 APRIL 1857

Secretary of State
Clarendon, Earl of
Permanent Under Secretary
Hammond, E.
Parliamentary Under Secretary
Shelburne, Earl of
Chief Clerk
Lenox Conyngham, G.
Senior Clerks
Ward, T. L.
Oom, A. K.
Murray, J.
Forster, H. F.
Coles, A. L.
Wellesley, R. G.
Spring Rice, Hon. T. C. W.
Alston, F. B.
Assistant Clerks
Wylde, W. H.
Ponsonby, Hon. S. C. B.
Hole, J. B.
Bidwell, J.
Morier, G.
Staveley, T. G.
Pennell, J. C.
Woodford, J. W. G.
Gifford, Hon. E. S.
First Class Junior Clerks
Synge, W. W. F.
Cavendish, F. W. H.
Wolff, H. D.
Vivian, Hon. H. C.
Dashwood, J. E. B.
Cowell, A. K.
Kennedy, C. M.
Lister, T. V.
Anderson, H. P.
Abbott, C. S. A.
Second Class Junior Clerks
Currie, P. H. W.
Vernon, G. R.
Crichton Stuart, H.
Stephens, F. S. M.
Hervey, H. A. W.
Clarke Jervoise, H. S. C.
Walsham, J.
Owen, W.
Eliot, Hon. H. C.
Third Class Junior Clerks
Buckley, V.
Crawford, O. J. F.
Warburton, J. W.
Farquharson, J. A.
Two vacancies
Clerks attached to Chief Clerk's Department
Scott, H. D.
Ayers, J.
Grey, T. B.
Sanders, H. W. (*Extra*)
Superintendent of Treaty Department
Bergne, J. B.
Clerk attached to Treaty Department
Bury, R.
Librarian
Hertslet, L.
Sub-Librarian
Hertslet, E.
Clerks attached to Librarian's Department
Sasse, F. R.
Green, A. S.
Irving, F.
Walmisley, A.
March, G. E.

Translator
Norris, E.
Précis Writer
Cavendish, F. W. H.
Private Secretary to Secretary of State
Ponsonby, Hon. S. C. B.

Office Keepers
Coxhead, G.
Tyler, J.
Greenall, W.
Rolfe, R.
Housekeeper
Watson, A.
Office Porters
Catchpole, J.
Mills, T.

Doorkeepers
Weller, J.
Haley, J.
Printer
Harrison, T. R.
Lamplighter and Coal Porter
Farmer, T.

Alphabetical List of Officials

Abbott, Charles Stuart Aubrey (succ. as 3rd Lord **Tenterden** 10 April 1870) *Extra Clerk* 1–10 April 1854 (FO 366/449 p. 154). *Assistant Junior Clerk* 10 April–1 July 1854 (ibid. p. 160; FO 366/384). *Junior Clerk* 1 July 1854–1 April 1857 (*FOL* (Aug. 1854), 9). *First Class Junior Clerk* 1 April 1857–1 Dec. 1866 (*FOL* (July 1857), 9). *Assistant Clerk* 1 Dec. 1866 (*FOL* (Jan. 1867), 7).

Précis Writer 6 July 1866–9 Dec. 1868 (FO 366/676 p. 112; FO 366/385).

Abercromby, Ralph *Précis Writer* 5 July 1827–12 Aug. 1828 (FO 366/673 p. 57; FO 366/381).

Aberdeen, George (Hamilton Gordon) 4th Earl of *Secretary of State* 30 May 1828–22 Nov. 1830 (*Times*, 31 May 1828; *London Gazette* no. 18474); 3 Sept. 1841–6 July 1846 (*Times*, 4 Sept. 1841; *London Gazette* no. 20014).

Adams, William Pitt *Assistant Junior Clerk* 5 April 1826–5 July 1830 (FO 366/381–2). *Junior Clerk* 5 July 1830–17 Nov. 1834 (FO 366/382). Left office 17 Nov. 1834 on app. as Secretary of Legation, Bogota (ibid.; FO 366/673 p. 248; *Dip. Rep.*, 39).

Addington, Henry Unwin *Permanent Under Secretary* 4 March 1842–9 April 1854 (FO 366/674 p. 162; FO 366/383–4). Ret. 9 April 1854 (FO 366/449 pp. 166–9, 183–4; FO 366/384).

Addison, Robert *Assistant Doorkeeper* 5 Jan. 1826–27 Aug. 1827 (FO 366/672 p. 452). Res. 27 Aug. 1827 (FO 366/673 p. 67).

Alexander, Raynsford Du Pré *Third Class Junior Clerk* 4 July 1857–1 Jan. 1860 (FO 366/449 p. 523; FO 366/384). *Second Class Junior Clerk* 1 Jan. 1860–6 Sept. 1864 (*FOL* (Jan. 1860), 9). Res. 6 Sept. 1864 (FO 366/675 p. 532; FO 366/385).

Alston, Francis Beilby *Assistant Junior Clerk* 15 Dec. 1839–29 Oct. 1841 (FO 366/673 p. 409; FO 366/382). *Junior Clerk* 29 Oct. 1841–14 Jan. 1849 (FO 366/382–3). *Second Class Clerk* 14 Jan. 1849–1 April 1857 (FO 366/383–4). *Senior Clerk* 1 April 1857–1 Dec. 1866 (*FOL* (July 1857), 9). *Chief Clerk* 1 Dec. 1866 (FO 366/676 pp. 133–5).

Ancell, Richard *Librarian and Keeper of the Papers* 5 Jan. 1801–5 Jan. 1810 (FO 366/1292, payment 10 Feb. 1802). Ret. 5 Jan. 1810 (FO 366/672 pp. 2–4).

Ancell, Thomas *Deputy Office Keeper* March 1782–*c.* 1787 (*Royal Kal.* (1783), 110; *1st Rept. on Fees*, 32). *Office Keeper c.* 1787–24 March 1795; probably app. 1787 in place of R. Turner; first occ. 1788 (*Royal Kal.* (1788), 104). D. 24 March 1795 (*Gent. Mag.* (1795), lxv (1), 352; FO 366/380).

Ancram, John William Robert (Kerr) *styled* Earl of *Private Secretary to Secretary of State* (Castlereagh) 5 July 1819–5 Jan. 1820 (FO 366/380).

Anderson, Henry Percy *Clerk* (*Slave Trade Dept.*) 18 Oct. 1852–1 April 1854 (FO 366/449 p. 58). *Assistant Junior Clerk* 1 April–1 July 1854 (ibid. p. 154; FO 366/384). *Junior Clerk* 1 July 1854–1 April 1857 (*FOL* (Aug. 1854), 9). *First Class Junior Clerk* 1 April 1857–4 June 1865 (*FOL* (July 1857), 9). *Assistant Clerk* 4 June 1865 (*FOL* (Jan. 1866), 9).

Anson, Thomas George (Anson) *styled* Viscount *Précis Writer* app. 9 July 1846 (FO 366/674 p. 439); pd. to 5 July 1847 (FO 366/383); remained in office without salary after election as M.P. July 1847 until *c.* April 1849 (ibid.).

Arbuthnot, Charles *Précis Writer* 29 Sept. 1793–25 March 1795 (Add. MS 58968 f. 99; FO 366/1292, payments 3 Nov. 1794, 14 March 1795). *Under Secretary* 8 Nov. 1803–5 June 1804 (FO 366/671 pp. 235, 252).

Ashburnham, Hon. Charles *Précis Writer* 12 Aug. 1828–27 Aug. 1829 (FO 366/381–2; FO 366/673 p. 100).

Aspain, Henry *Office Keeper* 8 March 1824–24 Sept. 1834 (FO 366/672 pp. 379, 385; FO 366/381–2). Left office 24 Sept. 1834 on app. as King's Home Service Messenger (FO 366/673 p. 236; FO 366/382).

Astley, Hugh Francis Lethbridge *Assistant Junior Clerk* 14 Dec. 1852–22 Aug. 1853 (FO 366/449 p. 60; FO 366/383). Res. 22 Aug. 1853 (FO 366/449 p. 82; FO 366/383).

Aust, George *Clerk* 27 March 1782–20 Feb. 1790 (FO 366/669, pt. i, p. 65). *Under Secretary* 20 Feb. 1790–5 Jan. 1796 (FO 366/670 pp. 16, 360).

Ayers, John *Extra Clerk* (*Chief Clerk's Dept.*) 9 Feb. 1852–1 July 1854 (FO 366/674 pp. 549–53). *Clerk* (*Chief Clerk's Dept.*) 1 July 1854 (FO 366/449 pp. 353–4).

Backhouse, George Canning *Assistant Junior Clerk* 24 May 1838–22 Nov. 1839 (FO 366/673 p. 363; FO 366/382). *Junior Clerk* 22 Nov. 1839–9 March 1844 (FO 366/382–3). *Second Class Clerk* 9 March 1844–15 Dec. 1852 (FO 366/383). Left office 15 Dec. 1852 on app. as Judge, Anglo-Spanish Commission for Suppression of Slave Trade, Havana (ibid.; *FOL* (1853), 14, 30).

Backhouse, John *Acting Under Secretary* 26 Oct. 1822–22 Jan. 1823 (FO 366/672 pp. 285, 298). *Permanent Under Secretary* 23 April 1827–5 April 1842 (FO 366/673 p. 33; FO 366/381–2). Ret. 5 April 1842 (FO 366/674 pp. 138–9; FO 366/382).

Bagot, Hon. Charles *Under Secretary* 19 Aug. 1807–16 Oct. 1809 (FO 366/671 pp. 338, 391).

Bagot, Ernest Alfred John *Clerk* (*Librarian's Dept.*) 12 May 1868 (FO 366/676 p. 266).

Bandinel, James *Clerk* 5 April 1799–28 March 1822 (FO 366/671 p. 137; FO 366/380). *Senior Clerk* 28 March 1822–12 Dec. 1845 (PC 2/204 p. 86; FO 366/381–3). Ret. 12 Dec. 1845 (FO 366/674 pp. 389–91; FO 366/383).

Superintendent of Slave Trade Dept. 5 Jan. 1824–12 Dec. 1845 (FO 83/40, 4 Dec. 1824).

Bankhead, Charles *Supernumerary Clerk* 24 Dec. 1814–5 July 1817 (FO 366/672 p. 91; FO 366/1292, payment 5 Jan. 1815). *Clerk* 5 July 1817–28 March 1822 (FO 366/380). *Junior Clerk* 28 March 1822–5 Jan. 1824 (PC 2/204 p. 86; FO 366/381). *Second Class Clerk* 5 Jan. 1824–5 Jan. 1826 (FO 366/381). Left office 5 Jan. 1826 on app. as Secretary of Legation, Washington (ibid.; *Dip. Rep.*, 188).

Clerk Assistant to Under Secretaries 10 Oct. 1823–5 Jan. 1825 (FO 366/381).

Barnett, Hamilton Brown *Temporary Clerk* (*Librarian's Dept.*) 1 July 1868 (FO 366/676 pp. 274, 340–5).

Barrington, Hon. Bernard Eric Edward *Third Class Junior Clerk* 7 Feb. 1867–3 July 1869 (FO 366/676 p. 131; FO 366/257). *Second Class Junior Clerk* 3 July 1869 (*FOL* (Jan. 1870), 5).

Private Secretary to Parliamentary Under Secretary (Otway) 12 Dec. 1868 (FO 366/676 p. 373).

Bartlett, Richard *Extra Clerk* 7 Feb. 1806–5 Jan. 1822 (FO 366/671 p. 301; FO

366/1292, payment 2 Aug. 1806). Left office 5 Jan. 1822 on app. as Consul, Corunna (FO 366/1292, payments 5 Jan., 6 April 1822; FO 83/1219 pp. 232–3).

Bathurst, Henry (Bathurst) 3rd Earl *Secretary of State* 11 Oct.–6 Dec. 1809 (FO 366/380; *London Gazette* no. 16305).

Batterbee, Thomas Owen *Office Keeper* 21 Aug. 1868 (FO 366/676 p. 332).

Bentinck *see* **Cavendish Bentinck**

Bergne, John Brodribb *Clerk (Treaty Dept.)* 5 Jan. 1817–1 July 1854 (FO 366/673 pp. 39–40; FO 366/382–4). *Superintendent of Treaty Dept.* 1 July 1854 (FO 366/449 pp. 353–4).

Bergne, John Henry Gibbs *Third Class Junior Clerk* 14 March 1861–4 June 1865 (FO 366/675 p. 299; FO 366/384–5). *Second Class Junior Clerk* 4 June 1865 (*FOL* (Jan. 1866), 9).

Bertie, Hon. Francis Leveson *Third Class Junior Clerk* 6 Nov. 1863–2 June 1867 (FO 366/675 p. 499; FO 366/384–5). *Second Class Junior Clerk* 2 June 1867 (*FOL* (March 1868), 7).

Bidwell, John *Extra Clerk* 5 July 1798–1 April 1799 (FO 366/1292, payments 25 Oct. 1798, 1 Feb. 1799). *Clerk* 1 April 1799–28 March 1822 (FO 366/671 pp. 117–18; FO 366/380). *Senior Clerk* 28 March 1822–30 Sept. 1851 (PC 2/204 p. 86; FO 366/381–3). Ret. 30 Sept. 1851 (FO 366/674 pp. 508–12; FO 366/383).

Assistant to Under Secretaries 2 Feb. 1824–5 Jan. 1826 (FO 366/672 p. 352; FO 366/381). *Superintendent of Consular Dept.* 5 Jan. 1826–30 Sept. 1851 (FO 366/672 pp. 429–32; FO 366/381–3).

Bidwell, John *Assistant Junior Clerk* 5 Jan. 1842–12 Dec. 1845 (FO 366/674 p. 157; FO 366/382–3). *Junior Clerk* 12 Dec. 1845–14 Dec. 1852 (FO 366/383). *Second Class Clerk* 14 Dec. 1852–1 April 1857 (*FOL* (1853), 9). *Assistant Clerk* 1 April 1857–1 April 1859 (*FOL* (July 1857), 9). *Senior Clerk* 1 April 1859 (*FOL* (July 1859), 9).

Précis Writer 14–28 Dec. 1852 (FO 366/449 p. 60; FO 366/383). *Private Secretary to Secretary of State* (Malmesbury) 26 Feb. 1858–18 June 1859 (FO 366/675 p. 9; FO 366/384).

Bidwell, Thomas *Clerk* 27 March 1782–18 April 1792 (FO 366/669, pt. i, p. 65). *Chief Clerk* 18 April 1792–28 Sept. 1817 (FO 366/670 p. 125). D. 28 Sept. 1817 (FO 366/380).

Bidwell, Thomas *Clerk* 20 Oct. 1790–28 March 1822 (FO 366/670 p. 61). *Senior Clerk* 28 March 1822–2 Feb. 1824 (PC 2/204 p. 86; FO 366/381). *Chief Clerk* 2 Feb. 1824–5 April 1841 (FO 366/672 p. 352). Ret. 5 April 1841 (FO 366/674 pp. 1–2, 48; FO 366/382).

Blackburn, John Edward *Assistant Junior Clerk* 17 Nov. 1834–5 July 1839 (FO 366/673 p. 248; FO 366/382). *Junior Clerk* 5 July 1839–29 Oct. 1841 (FO 366/382). *Second Class Clerk* 29 Oct. 1841–17 Nov. 1851 (FO 366/382–3). Ret. 17 Nov. 1851 (FO 366/674 pp. 517–20; FO 366/383).

Bode, — *Clerk (Treaty Dept.)* 29 June–*c.* 17 Oct. 1846 (FO 366/674 p. 438). Res. by 17 Oct. 1846 (ibid. p. 445).

Boileau, John Elliot *Assistant Private Secretary to Secretary of State* (Russell) 29 Dec. 1852–21 Feb. 1853 (*FOL* (Jan. 1854), 52).

Bouverie *see* **Pleydell Bouverie**

Brabazon, Reginald (Brabazon) *styled* Lord *Third Class Junior Clerk* 30 July 1863–3 Jan. 1867 (FO 366/675 p. 456; FO 366/384–5). *Second Class Junior Clerk*

3 Jan. 1867–7 June 1868 (*FOL* (March 1868), 7). Left office 7 June 1868 on app. as Third Secretary, Berlin (FO 366/385; *FOL* (Jan. 1869), 33, 64).

Bristol, Earl of *see* **Hervey,** Lord

Broughton, Bryan *Clerk* 27 March 1782–19 Jan. 1788 (FO 366/669, pt. i, p. 65). Res. 19 Jan. 1788 (Add. MS 28063 f. 31).

Broughton, Charles Rivington *Clerk* 22 April 1788–28 March 1822 (FO 366/669, pt. ii, p. 201). *Senior Clerk* 28 March 1822–5 Jan. 1824 (PC 2/204 p. 86; FO 366/381). Ret. 5 Jan. 1824 (FO 366/672 pp. 350–1; FO 366/381).

Browne, John Henry Torrens Temple *Clerk* (*Slave Trade Dept.*) 16 June 1834–8 April 1835 (FO 84/162 ff. 157–8). Dis. 8 April 1835 (FO 84/184 ff. 31–2). *Extra Clerk* 13 Dec. 1837–14 March 1838 (FO 366/673 p. 336). *Clerk* (*Slave Trade Dept.*) 14 March 1838–*c*. Nov. 1840 (ibid. p. 349; FO 84/261 ff. 214–16). Left office *c*. Nov. 1840 (FO 84/342 f. 302).

Bruce, Hon. James *Précis Writer* 10 Oct. 1797–10 July 1798 (FO 366/671 p. 45; FO 366/380). D. 10 July 1798 (*Gent. Mag.* (1798), lxviii (2), 635).

Buckley, Victor *Assistant Junior Clerk* 12 Jan.–1 April 1857 (FO 366/449 p. 457; FO 366/384). *Third Class Junior Clerk* 1 April–7 Dec. 1857 (FO 366/384). *Second Class Junior Clerk* 7 Dec. 1857–1 Oct. 1863 (*FOL* (Jan. 1858), 9). *First Class Junior Clerk* 1 Oct. 1863 (*FOL* (Jan. 1864), 9).

Bulgin, Abraham *Office Keeper* 10 Oct. 1795–3 Oct. 1797 (FO 366/380). D. 3 Oct. 1797 (Prob. 11/1296 f. 629).

Burges, James Bland *Under Secretary* 22 Aug. 1789–16 Oct. 1795 (FO 366/669, pt. ii, p. 237; FO 366/670 p. 339).

Burman, Henry *Doorkeeper* 10 Oct. 1810–26 Feb. 1812 (FO 366/1292, payment 5 Jan. 1811). *Office Keeper* 26 Feb. 1812–5 April 1826 (FO 366/380–1). Ret. 5 April 1826 (FO 366/673 p. 1; FO 366/381).

Bury, Richard Employed in Foreign Office from 23 Dec. 1844 (*FOL* (Jan. 1855), 9). *Clerk* (*Treaty Dept.*) 12 Nov. 1852 (FO 366/449 pp. 59, 353–4).

Byng, Frederick Gerald (*styled* Hon. 14 Dec. 1812) *Clerk* 23 Jan. 1801–28 March 1822 (FO 366/671 p. 154). *Second Class Clerk* 28 March 1822–5 Jan. 1824 (PC 2/204 p. 86; FO 366/381). *Senior Clerk* 5 Jan. 1824–5 April 1839 (FO 366/381–2). Ret. 5 April 1839 (FO 366/673 pp. 373–5; FO 366/382).

Superintendent of Foreign Ministers' Accounts 5 Jan. 1827–5 April 1839 (FO 366/673 pp. 28–9; FO 366/381–2).

Cade, Joseph *Acting Supernumerary Clerk* 3 May 1819–10 Oct. 1823 (FO 366/672 p. 175). Left office 10 Oct. 1823 on app. as Paid Attaché, Commission to Colombia (FO 366/329 f. 28).

Canning, Charles John (Canning) 2nd Viscount *Parliamentary Under Secretary* 4 Sept. 1841–26 Jan. 1846 (FO 366/674 p. 143; FO 366/382–3).

Canning, George *Under Secretary* 5 Jan. 1796–1 April 1799 (FO 366/670 p. 360; FO 366/671 p. 115). *Secretary of State* 25 March 1807–11 Oct. 1809 (*London Gazette* no. 16014; FO 366/380); 16 Sept. 1822–30 April 1827 (*London Gazette* no. 17853; FO 366/381).

Canning, Stratford *Précis Writer* 5 July 1807–5 Jan. 1809 (FO 366/380).

Cannon, Charles *Translator* 1 April 1866 (FO 366/676 pp. 97, 100–1; FO 366/385).

Carmarthen, Francis Godolphin (Osborne) *styled* Marquess of (succ. as 5th Duke of Leeds 23 March 1789) *Secretary of State* 23 Dec. 1783–21 April 1791 (T 52/73 p. 55; *London Gazette* no. 12503; T 53/60 p. 165).

Carpenter, Percy *Temporary Clerk* (*Librarian's Dept.*) 29 Jan. 1862 (FO 366/675 p. 406; FO 366/257–8).

Carter, Richard *Clerk* 27 March 1782–*c.* 1785 (FO 366/669, pt. i, p. 65). Probably left office in 1785; occ. in *Royal Kal.* (1785), 104; not included in list of Clerks, Michaelmas 1785 (FO 366/669, pt. ii, p. 132).

Cartwright, Thomas *Précis Writer* 5 July 1817–5 Jan. 1821 (FO 366/380).

Casamajor, Justinian *Clerk* 18 Aug. 1797–5 April 1799 (FO 366/671 p. 42). Left office 5 April 1799 on app. as Secretary of Legation, St. Petersburg (FO 366/380; *London Gazette* no. 15123).

Castlereagh, Robert (Stewart) *styled* Viscount (succ. as 2nd Marquess of **Londonderry** 6 April 1821) *Secretary of State* 28 Feb. 1812–12 Aug. 1822 (FO 366/672 p. 42; *London Gazette* no. 16580). D. 12 Aug. 1822.

Catchpole, George *Assistant Doorkeeper* 19 Aug. 1863–11 March 1868 (FO 366/675 p. 475). *Office Keeper* 11 March 1868–27 April 1869 (FO 366/676 p. 263). Left office 27 April 1869 on app. as Queen's Home Service Messenger (ibid. p. 430; FO 366/257).

Catchpole, John *Assistant Doorkeeper* 27 Dec. 1841–6 July 1843 (FO 366/674 p. 150). *Head Office Porter* 6 July 1843 (ibid. p. 238).

Cavendish, Francis William Henry *Assistant Junior Clerk* 9 May 1848–14 Dec. 1852 (FO 366/674 p. 465; FO 366/383). *Junior Clerk* 14 Dec. 1852–1 July 1854 (*FOL* (1853), 9). *Second Class Clerk* 1 July 1854–1 April 1857 (*FOL* (Aug. 1854), 9). *First Class Junior Clerk* 1 April 1857–1 Jan. 1859 (FO 366/384). *Assistant Clerk* 1 Jan. 1859–30 Sept. 1863 (*FOL* (Jan. 1859), 9). Ret. 30 Sept. 1863 (FO 366/675 pp. 507–8, 516; FO 366/384).

Précis Writer 29 Dec. 1852–8 Dec. 1857 (FO 366/449 pp. 65, 551; FO 366/383–4).

Cavendish, Hon. Henry Anson (succ. as 4th Lord **Waterpark** 31 March 1863) *Third Class Junior Clerk* 19 Jan. 1860–6 May 1863 (FO 366/675 p. 202; FO 366/384). Res. 6 May 1863 (FO 366/675 p. 456: FO 366/384).

Cavendish Bentinck, Lord William George Frederick *Private Secretary to Secretary of State* (Canning) 10 Oct. 1822–5 April 1824 (FO 366/381).

Chaplin, Thomas *Office Porter* occ. 15 Dec. 1785 (*1st Rept. on Fees*, 32).

Cheese, Ann *Housekeeper* probably app. 1783 in place of Southcott; had been in office 'about two years' 15 Dec. 1785 (*1st Rept. on Fees*, 33). Pd. to 5 Jan. 1805 (FO 366/380).

Christopher, George *Office Keeper* 5 Sept. 1853–30 Jan. 1857 (FO 366/449 p. 84; FO 366/384). Left office 30 Jan. 1857 on app. as Queen's Home Service Messenger (FO 366/449 p. 488; FO 366/384).

Clanricarde, Ulick John (De Burgh) 1st Marquess of *Under Secretary* 2 Jan. 1826–12 Aug. 1827 (FO 366/672 p. 442; FO 366/381).

Clanwilliam, Richard Charles Francis Christian (Meade) 3rd Earl of *Private Secretary to Secretary of State* (Castlereagh/Londonderry) 5 July 1817–5 July 1819 (FO 366/380); 5 Jan. 1820–29 Jan. 1822 (ibid.). *Under Secretary* 30 Jan. 1822–5 Jan. 1823 (FO 366/672 p. 257; FO 366/381).

Acting Under Secretary 17 May 1820–July 1821 (FO 366/672 p. 185; FO 366/329 f. 34).

Clarendon, George William Frederick (Villiers) 4th Earl of *Secretary of State* 21 Feb. 1853–26 Feb. 1858 (*Times*, 22 Feb. 1853; *London Gazette* no. 21413); 3 Nov. 1865–6 July 1866 (*Times*, 4 Nov. 1865; *London Gazette* no. 23034); 9 Dec. 1868–27

June 1870 (*Times*, 10 Dec. 1868; *London Gazette* no. 23449). D. 27 June 1870.

Clarke Jervoise, Harry Samuel Cumming *Assistant Junior Clerk* 16 Aug. 1854–1 Dec. 1856 (FO 366/449 p. 355; FO 366/384). *Junior Clerk* 1 Dec. 1856–1 April 1857 (FO 366/384). *Second Class Junior Clerk* 1 April 1857–1 Jan. 1860 (ibid.). *First Class Junior Clerk* 1 Jan. 1860 (*FOL* (Jan. 1860), 9).

Private Secretary to Parliamentary Under Secretary (Egerton) 6 July 1866–9 Dec. 1868 (FO 366/676 p. 115; FO 366/385).

Cockburn, Alexander *Clerk* 5 Jan. 1795–5 Jan. 1799 (FO 366/380). Left office 5 Jan. 1799 on app. as Agent and Consul General, Lower Saxony (ibid.; FO 366/329 f. 35; *London Gazette* no. 15105).

Cockerell, William Acland *Third Class Junior Clerk* 27 Jan. 1860–7 Sept. 1864 (FO 366/675 p. 211; FO 366/384). *Second Class Junior Clerk* 7 Sept. 1864 (*FOL* (Jan. 1866), 9).

Cocking, Henry Valentine *Office Keeper* 24 Sept. 1834–1 Oct. 1843 (FO 366/673 p. 236; FO 366/382–3). Salary ceased 1 Oct. 1843 (FO 366/383); app. Queen's Home Service Messenger 28 Nov. 1843 (*FOL* (Jan. 1874), 75).

Coles, Augustus Leopold *Assistant Junior Clerk* 2 Nov. 1835–5 July 1839 (FO 366/673 p. 290; FO 366/382). *Junior Clerk* 5 July 1839–7 Aug. 1843 (FO 366/382–3). *Second Class Clerk* 7 Aug. 1843–1 July 1854 (FO 366/383–4). *Senior Clerk* 1 July 1854–9 Oct. 1866 (*FOL* (Aug. 1854), 9). Ret. 9 Oct. 1866 (FO 366/676 pp. 125–7, 150; FO 366/385).

Conway, John *Office Keeper* 22 Jan. 1807–25 Feb. 1812 (FO 366/671 p. 314). D. 25 Feb. 1812 (FO 366/672 pp. 37–8).

Conyngham, Lord Francis Nathaniel (*styled* Earl of **Mount Charles** 26 Dec. 1824) *Under Secretary* 6 Jan. 1823–17 March 1825 (FO 366/672 pp. 292, 400).

Conyngham *see also* **Lenox Conyngham**

Cook, John *Office Porter* first occ. 1791 (*Royal Kal.* (1791), 104). Left office *c.* June 1795 (FO 366/1292, payment 21 July 1795).

Cooke, Edward *Under Secretary* 28 Feb. 1812–5 July 1817 (FO 366/672 pp. 34–5, 144; FO 366/380).

Coral, Francis *Office Keeper* 5 Jan. 1797–5 Jan. 1812 (FO 366/380). Ret. 5 Jan. 1812 (FO 366/672 pp. 22–4, 27; FO 366/380).

Corry *see* **Lowry Corry**

Cowell (from 29 Dec. 1857 **Cowell Stepney**), Arthur Keppel *Assistant Junior Clerk* 26 Sept. 1852–1 July 1854 (FO 366/449 p. 54; FO 366/383–4). *Junior Clerk* 1 July 1854–1 April 1857 (*FOL* (Aug. 1854), 9). *First Class Junior Clerk* 1 April 1857–1 Jan. 1862 (*FOL* (July 1857), 9). *Assistant Clerk* 1 Jan. 1862 (*FOL* (Jan. 1862), 9).

Cowper, Hon. Charles Spencer *Assistant Junior Clerk* 14 Nov. 1834–5 July 1839 (FO 366/673 p. 247; FO 366/382). *Junior Clerk* 5 July–22 Nov. 1839 (FO 366/382). Left office 22 Nov. 1839 on app. as Secretary of Legation, Florence (ibid.; *Dip. Rep.*, 175).

Private Secretary to Secretary of State (Palmerston) 11 May 1835–5 Jan. 1840 (FO 366/673 p. 283; FO 366/382).

Coxhead, George *Office Keeper* 2 Oct. 1843 (FO 366/674 pp. 264, 401).

Crawford, Oswald John Frederick *Assistant Junior Clerk* 23 Jan.–1 April 1857 (FO 366/449 p. 462; FO 366/384). *Third Class Junior Clerk* 1 April 1857–1 Jan. 1859 (FO 366/384). *Second Class Junior Clerk* 1 Jan. 1859–4 June 1865 (*FOL* (Jan.

1859), 9). *First Class Junior Clerk* 4 June 1865–2 Jan. 1867 (*FOL* (Jan. 1866), 9). Left office 2 Jan. 1867 on app. as Consul, Oporto (FO 366/385; *FOL* (March 1868), 34, 79).

Crichton Stuart, Herbert *Assistant Junior Clerk* 7 May 1854–1 Jan. 1855 (FO 366/449 p. 163; FO 366/384). *Junior Clerk* 1 Jan. 1855–1 April 1857 (*FOL* (June 1855), 9). *Second Class Junior Clerk* 1 April 1857–1 April 1859 (FO 366/384). *First Class Junior Clerk* 1 April 1859–29 June 1870 (FO 366/384–5; FO 366/257–8). Ret. 29 June 1870 (FO 366/677 pp. 13–14; FO 366/258).

Currie, Philip Henry Wodehouse *Assistant Junior Clerk* 10 April–1 Oct. 1854 (FO 366/449 p. 162; FO 366/384). *Junior Clerk* 1 Oct. 1854–1 April 1857 (*FOL* (Jan. 1855), 9). *Second Class Junior Clerk* 1 April–7 Dec. 1857 (FO 366/384). *First Class Junior Clerk* 7 Dec. 1857–1 Jan. 1868 (*FOL* (Jan. 1858), 9). *Assistant Clerk* 1 Jan. 1868 (*FOL* (March 1868), 7).

Précis Writer 9 Dec. 1857–25 Feb. 1858 (FO 366/449 p. 551; FO 366/384).

Dakin, William *Doorkeeper* probably app. 1786; first occ. 1787 (*Royal Kal.* (1787), 104); had been in office 'near 25 years' 8 Sept. 1810 (FO 366/672 pp. 10–11). Ret. 10 Oct. 1810 (ibid. pp. 12, 20; FO 366/1292, payment 27 May 1811).

Dalbertanson, Charles Ildefonse *Assistant Doorkeeper* 15 March 1862–31 July 1863 (FO 366/675 p. 392). *Office Keeper* 31 July 1863 (ibid. p. 475).

Dallas, George Edward *Third Class Junior Clerk* 1 Dec. 1863–1 Jan. 1868 (FO 366/675 p. 503; FO 366/384–5). *Second Class Junior Clerk* 1 Jan. 1868 (*FOL* (March 1868), 7).

Dashwood, James Edward Bateman *Clerk* (*Slave Trade Dept.*) 1 April–14 Aug. 1852 (FO 366/449 p. 6). *Assistant Junior Clerk* 14 Aug. 1852–1 July 1854 (ibid. p. 48; FO 366/383–4). *Junior Clerk* 1 July 1854–13 March 1857 (*FOL* (Aug. 1854), 9). *Second Class Clerk* 13 March–1 April 1857 (FO 366/384). *First Class Junior Clerk* 1 April 1857–1 Jan. 1860 (ibid.). *Assistant Clerk* 1 Jan. 1860 (*FOL* (Jan. 1860), 9).

Précis Writer 26 Feb. 1858–18 June 1859 (FO 366/675 p. 9; FO 366/384).

Dashwood, William John Popple *Clerk* (*Slave Trade Dept.*) 21 Nov. 1845–31 March 1852 (FO 366/674 p. 396). Left office 31 March 1852 (FO 366/383).

Dassonville, Mary *Housekeeper* 5 July 1806–17 May 1814 (FO 366/671 p. 304). D. 17 May 1814 (FO 366/380).

Dawkins, Clinton George Augustus *Extra Clerk* 27 Aug. 1829–26 April 1831 (FO 366/673 p. 102). *Assistant Junior Clerk* 26 April 1831–5 April 1838 (ibid. p. 165; FO 366/382). *Junior Clerk* 5 April 1838–21 Aug. 1841 (FO 366/382). *Second Class Clerk* 21 Aug. 1841–25 June 1846 (FO 366/382–3). Left office 25 June 1846 on app. as Consul General, Lombardy (FO 366/505, 26 June 1846; FO 366/383).

Acting Précis Writer 27 Aug. 1829–26 April 1831 (FO 366/673 pp. 101, 138, 159, 165; FO 366/382). *Private Secretary to Secretary of State* (Aberdeen) 3 Sept. 1841–5 July 1846 (FO 366/674 p. 144; FO 366/382–3).

Dickens, James *Extra Clerk* pd. from *c.* Oct. 1795 to 5 July 1798 (FO 366/1292, payments 1 June 1796, 16 July 1798).

Douglas, Andrew Snape *Assistant Précis Writer* Nov. 1807–Jan. 1809 (FO 366/329 f. 44).

Dowling, Daniel Morton *Clerk* (*Slave Trade Dept.*) 20 Aug. 1841–20 Oct. 1845 (FO 366/674 p. 34). Res. 20 Oct. 1845 (ibid. pp. 387–8).

Dudley and Ward, John William (Ward) 4th Viscount (cr. Earl of **Dudley** 5 Oct.

1827) *Secretary of State* 30 April 1827–30 May 1828 (*Times*, 1 May 1827; *London Gazette* no. 18357).

Dunglas, Cospatrick Alexander (Home) *styled* Lord *Précis Writer* 5 July 1824–5 July 1827 (FO 366/381). *Under Secretary* 9 June 1828–22 Nov. 1830 (FO 366/673 pp. 72, 150).

Eddisbury, Lord *see* **Stanley,** Hon. Edward John

Edwardes, Hon. Richard *Assistant Junior Clerk* 23 April 1827–17 Aug. 1832 (FO 366/673 pp. 34–5; FO 366/381–2). Res. 17 Aug. 1832 (FO 366/673 p. 216; FO 366/382).

Egerton, Edward Christopher *Parliamentary Under Secretary* 6 July 1866–9 Dec. 1868 (FO 366/676 pp. 113–14; FO 366/385).

Eliot, Hon. Henry Cornwallis *Assistant Junior Clerk* 28 Jan. 1855–1 April 1857 (FO 366/449 p. 370; FO 366/384). *Second Class Junior Clerk* 1 April 1857–2 Aug. 1863 (*FOL* (July 1857), 9). *First Class Junior Clerk* 2 Aug. 1863 (*FOL* (Jan. 1864), 9).

Eliot, Hon. William *Under Secretary* 5 June 1804–25 Jan. 1805 (FO 366/671 pp. 252, 265).

Elliot, Hon. George Francis Stewart *Private Secretary to Secretary of State* (Russell) 18 June 1859–2 Nov. 1865 (FO 366/675 p. 170; FO 366/384–5).

Elliot, Hon. Henry George *Précis Writer* 20 April 1840–3 Sept. 1841 (FO 366/673 p. 483; FO 366/382).

Farmer, Thomas *Lamplighter and Coal Porter* 15 Oct. 1852 (FO 366/449 p. 57).

Farquharson, John Atholl *Assistant Junior Clerk* 21 Feb.–1 April 1857 (FO 366/449 p. 461; FO 366/384). *Third Class Junior Clerk* 1 April 1857–1 June 1859 (FO 366/384). *Second Class Junior Clerk* 1 June 1859–3 Jan. 1867 (*FOL* (July 1859), 9). *First Class Junior Clerk* 3 Jan. 1867 (*FOL* (March 1868), 7).

Fisher, Edward *Under Secretary* 25 Sept. 1800–20 Feb. 1801 (FO 366/671 p. 146; FO 366/380).

Fitzgerald *see* **Vesey Fitzgerald**

Fitzharris, James Edward (Harris) *styled* Viscount *Under Secretary* 30 March–19 Aug. 1807 (FO 366/671 pp. 319, 338).

Flint, Charles William *Clerk* probably app. in 1794; in office by 29 Oct. 1794 (Add. MS 59229 ff. 102–4). Salary ceased 5 July 1798 on app. as Superintendent of Aliens (FO 366/380; FO 366/671 pp. 64–5; HO 38/7 pp. 573–5).

Forbes, John *Private Secretary to Secretary of State* (Wellesley) pd. from 5 Jan. 1810 to 27 Feb. 1812 (FO 366/380).

Fordwich, George Augustus Frederick (Cowper) *styled* Viscount *Parliamentary Under Secretary* 13–17 Nov. 1834 (FO 366/673 p. 245; FO 366/382).

Forster, Henry Francis *Extra Clerk* 11 Jan. 1828–27 Aug. 1829 (FO 366/673 p. 66). *Assistant Junior Clerk* 27 Aug. 1829–10 Oct. 1835 (ibid. p. 96; FO 366/382). *Junior Clerk* 10 Oct. 1835–16 Aug. 1841 (FO 366/382). *Second Class Clerk* 16 Aug. 1841–10 April 1854 (FO 366/394, 16 Aug. 1841; FO 366/382–4). *Senior Clerk* 10 April 1854–1 Aug. 1863 (*FOL* (Aug. 1854), 9). D. 1 Aug. 1863 (*FOL* (Jan. 1864), 165).

Forsyth, William *Assistant Doorkeeper* 12 Dec. 1845–*c.* 9 Oct. 1849 (FO 366/674 p. 406). Left office by 9 Oct. 1849 (app. of Maulden).

Foster, Arthur *Clerk* (*Chief Clerk's Dept.*) 1 April 1868 (FO 366/676 pp. 236, 270–1).

Fox, Hon. Charles James *Secretary of State* 27 March–4 July 1782 (T 52/71 p. 336; *London Gazette* no. 12282); 2 April–19 Dec. 1783 (T 52/73 p. 55; *London Gazette* no. 12428); 7 Feb.–13 Sept. 1806 (FO 366/380; *London Gazette* no. 15887). D. 13 Sept. 1806 (*Gent. Mag.* (1806), lxxvi (2), 883).

Fox Strangways, Hon. William Thomas Horner *Parliamentary Under Secretary* 15 Aug. 1835–6 March 1840 (FO 366/673 p. 288; FO 366/382).

Francklin, George Fairfax *Extra Clerk* (*Chief Clerk's Dept.*) 6 Jan. 1827–18 April 1835 (FO 366/673 p. 32). *Clerk* (*Consular Dept.*) 18 April 1835–24 July 1839 (ibid. p. 279). Res. 24 July 1839 (ibid. p. 393; FO 366/228, account for year ending 31 March 1840).

Fraser, Hanson Werry *Temporary Clerk* (*Librarian's Dept.*) 15 April 1869 (FO 366/676 p. 416).

Fraser, William *Under Secretary* 27 March 1782–*c.* 22 Aug. 1789 (FO 366/669, pt. i, p. 65). Left office by 22 Aug. 1789 (app. of Burges).

Frere, George *Clerk* (*Slave Trade Dept.*) 5 Dec. 1826–20 Nov. 1842 (FO 96/28/1 ff. 3–4). Left office 20 Nov. 1842 on app. as Commissioner, Anglo-Portuguese Commission for Suppression of Slave Trade, Cape of Good Hope (FO 366/383; FO 83/892 pp. 145–55). *Temporary Clerk* (*Librarian's Dept.*) 1 July 1868 (FO 366/676 pp. 267, 340–5).

Frere, John Hookham *Under Secretary* 1 April 1799–25 Sept. 1800 (FO 366/671 pp. 115, 146).

Fullerton, William Granville *Assistant Private Secretary to Secretary of State* (Clarendon) 12 Feb.–29 May 1855 (*FOL* (June 1855), 71). D. 29 May 1855 (ibid.).

Garrod, Joseph *Lamplighter and Coal Porter* 10 Oct. 1812–6 May 1817 (FO 366/1292, payment 5 Jan. 1813). Left office 6 May 1817 (ibid., payment 6 May 1817).

Gifford, Hon. Edward Scott *Assistant Junior Clerk* 5 Feb. 1846–1 Oct. 1851 (FO 366/674 p. 420; FO 366/383). *Junior Clerk* 1 Oct. 1851–1 July 1854 (FO 366/383–4). *Second Class Clerk* 1 July 1854–1 April 1857 (*FOL* (Aug. 1854), 9). *Assistant Clerk* 1 April 1857–1 Jan. 1868 (*FOL* (July 1857), 9). *Senior Clerk* 1 Jan. 1868 (*FOL* (March 1868), 7).

Gladwell, William *Clerk* (*Consular Dept.*) 16 Nov. 1860–30 June 1861 (FO 366/675 p. 284). Salary ceased 30 June 1861 (ibid. p. 375).

Goddard, Charles *Private Secretary to Secretary of State* (Grenville) 5 Jan. 1795–5 Jan. 1796 (FO 366/380).

Gordon *see* **Hamilton Gordon**

Gordon Lennox, Lord Henry George Charles *Précis Writer* 18 Feb. 1845–5 Feb. 1846 (FO 366/674 pp. 375, 421; FO 366/383).

Gower *see* **Leveson Gower**

Gracewood, Andrew *Doorkeeper* 5 July 1815–5 Jan. 1851 (FO 366/1292, payment 11 Oct. 1815). D. 5 Jan. 1851 (FO 366/383).

Graham, Arthur *Doorkeeper* 26 Feb. 1812–*c.* 17 June 1815 (FO 366/1292, payment 2 April 1812). D. by 17 June 1815 (Prob. 11/1569 f. 311).

Graham, David *Clerk* 18 Oct. 1805–5 July 1817 (FO 366/671 p. 279). Ret. 5 July 1817 (FO 366/672 pp. 141, 145; FO 366/380).

Assistant Précis Writer 1 Jan. 1814–5 Jan. 1817 (FO 366/672 p. 88; FO 366/1292, payments 21 July 1814, 5 June 1817).

Grantham, Thomas (Robinson) 2nd Lord *Secretary of State* 10 July 1782–2 April 1783 (T 52/71 p. 400; *London Gazette* no. 12314).

Granville, Earl *see* **Leveson**, Lord

Green, Alfred Scrimshire *Temporary Clerk* (*Librarian's Dept.*) 19 Dec. 1844–1 July 1854 (FO 366/674 p. 370). *Clerk* (*Librarian's Dept.*) 1 July 1854–17 Jan. 1859 (FO 366/449 pp. 353–4). *Sub-Librarian* 17 Jan. 1859 (FO 366/675 p. 55).

Greenall, William *Deputy Office Porter* had been in office 'for a number of years' July 1843 (FO 366/393, 19 July 1843). *Assistant Doorkeeper* 6 July 1843–12 Dec. 1845 (FO 366/674 p. 245). *Office Keeper* 12 Dec. 1845–20 April 1864 (ibid. p. 401; FO 366/384–5). D. 20 April 1864 (FO 366/385).

Grenville, William Wyndham (Grenville) 1st Lord *Secretary of State* 29 April 1791–20 Feb. 1801 (Historical Manuscripts Commission, *14th Rept.*, *Appendix*, pt. v, 60; FO 366/380).

Greville, Algernon Frederick *Private Secretary to Secretary of State* (Wellington) 17 Nov. 1834–17 April 1835 (FO 366/673 p. 264; FO 366/382).

Greville, Henry William *Précis Writer* 17 Nov. 1834–7 April 1835 (FO 366/673 p. 264; FO 366/382).

Grey, Thomas Belgrave *Clerk* (*Chief Clerk's Dept.*) 11 July 1854–17 April 1865 (FO 366/449 p. 355). Dis. 17 April 1865 (FO 366/676 p. 35).

Haley, John *Assistant Doorkeeper* 1 Jan. 1855–21 Oct. 1861 (FO 366/449 p. 377; FO 366/384). *Office Keeper* 21 Oct. 1861–8 March 1868 (FO 366/675 p. 374). D. 8 March 1868 (*FOL* (March 1868), 102).

Hall, Robert King *Messenger* (*Librarian's Dept.*) 5 July 1869 (FO 366/676 p. 471).

Hamilton, William John *Précis Writer* 5 April–21 Nov. 1830 (FO 366/673 p. 138; FO 366/382).

Hamilton, William Richard *Précis Writer* 5 April 1804–6 March 1806 (FO 366/380). *Under Secretary* 16 Oct. 1809–29 Jan. 1822 (FO 366/671 p. 391; FO 366/380).
Private Secretary to Secretary of State (Harrowby) probably app. May 1804; pd. from 5 April to 5 July 1804 (FO 366/380).

Hamilton Gordon, Hon. Alexander *Précis Writer* 25 Nov. 1843–17 Feb. 1845 (FO 366/674 p. 246; FO 366/383).

Hamilton Gordon, Hon. Arthur *Assistant Private Secretary to Secretary of State* (Aberdeen) 3 Sept. 1841–5 July 1846 (*FOL* (Jan. 1854), 55).

Hammond, Edmund *Assistant Junior Clerk* 30 April 1824–5 Jan. 1825 (FO 366/672 pp. 377–8; FO 366/381). *Junior Clerk* 5 Jan. 1825–5 July 1830 (FO 366/381–2). *Second Class Clerk* 5 July 1830–21 Aug. 1841 (FO 366/382). *Senior Clerk* 21 Aug. 1841–10 April 1854 (FO 366/382–4). *Permanent Under Secretary* 10 April 1854 (FO 366/449 p. 158).
Clerk Assistant to Under Secretaries 26 April 1836–21 Aug. 1841 (FO 366/673 p. 314; FO 366/382).

Hammond, George *Under Secretary* 16 Oct. 1795–20 Feb. 1806 (FO 366/670 p. 339; FO 366/380); 30 March 1807–11 Nov. 1809 (FO 366/671 p. 319; FO 366/380).

Hamond, Horace *Précis Writer* 27 Feb.–31 March 1852 (FO 366/449 p. 4; FO 366/383).

Hansen, Christian Robert Buckman *Office Keeper* 21 Aug. 1868 (FO 366/676 p. 333).

Harris, George *Private Secretary to Secretary of State* (Malmesbury) 27 Feb.–28 Dec. 1852 (FO 366/449 p. 4; FO 366/383).

Harrison, James *Printer* 15 May 1800–20 March 1847 (FO 366/1292, payment 6 Nov. 1800). D. 20 March 1847 (FO 366/383).

Harrison, Thomas *Printer* 6 May 1869 (FO 366/676 pp. 435–6).

Harrison, Thomas Richard *Printer* 23 March 1847–29 April 1869 (FO 366/674 p. 449). D. 29 April 1869 (FO 366/676 pp. 433–4).

Harrowby, Lord *see* **Ryder,** Hon. Dudley

Hawkesbury, Robert Banks (Jenkinson) *styled* Lord *Secretary of State* 20 Feb. 1801–12 May 1804 (FO 366/380; *London Gazette* no. 15338).

Hay, James William *Clerk* 17 Oct. 1788–5 July 1805 (FO 366/669, pt. ii, p. 216). Ret. 5 July 1805 (FO 366/671 pp. 271–2; FO 366/380).

Hertslet, Edward *Temporary Clerk* (*Librarian's Dept.*) 8 Jan. 1842–28 Aug. 1844 (FO 366/674 p. 156). *Clerk* (*Librarian's Dept.*) 28 Aug. 1844–1 April 1855 (ibid. p. 303). *Sub-Librarian* 1 April 1855–19 Nov. 1857 (FO 366/449 p. 378; FO 366/384). *Librarian and Keeper of the Papers* 19 Nov. 1857 (FO 366/449 p. 544).

Hertslet, Edward Cecil *Clerk* (*Chief Clerk's Dept.*) 9 Sept. 1868 (FO 366/676 p. 278).

Hertslet, James *Sub-Librarian* 29 March 1811–31 March 1855 (FO 366/672 p. 16). Ret. 31 March 1855 (FO 366/449 pp. 380–7; FO 366/384).

Hertslet, Lewis *Sub-Librarian* 5 Feb. 1801–6 Jan. 1810 (FO 366/671 p. 396). *Librarian and Keeper of the Papers* 6 Jan. 1810–19 Nov. 1857 (FO 366/672 p. 5). Ret. 19 Nov. 1857 (FO 366/449 pp. 538, 543a; FO 366/384).

Hertslet, Reginald Henry *Temporary Clerk* (*Librarian's Dept.*) 20 May 1870 (FO 366/677 p. 12).

Hervey, Frederick William (Hervey) *styled* Lord (succ. as 5th Earl of **Bristol** 8 July 1803) *Under Secretary* 20 Feb. 1801–5 Aug. 1803 (FO 366/671 pp. 167–8, 235; FO 366/380).

Hervey, Henry Arthur William *Assistant Junior Clerk* 7 May 1854–1 Dec. 1856 (FO 366/449 p. 165; FO 366/384). *Junior Clerk* 1 Dec. 1856–1 April 1857 (FO 366/384). *Second Class Junior Clerk* 1 April 1857–28 July 1859 (ibid.). *First Class Junior Clerk* 28 July 1859 (*FOL* (July 1859), 9).

Précis Writer 3 Nov. 1865–5 July 1866 (FO 366/676 p. 77; FO 366/385); 10 Dec. 1868 (FO 366/676 p. 370; FO 366/677 p. 23).

Hervey, Hon. William (*styled* Lord William 30 June 1826) *Assistant Junior Clerk* 21 Jan. 1825–5 July 1826 (FO 366/672 p. 397; FO 366/381). *Junior Clerk* 5 July 1826–5 Jan. 1828 (FO 366/381). Left office 5 Jan. 1828 on app. as Paid Attaché, Vienna (ibid.; FO 366/329 f. 70).

Hill, Lord Arthur Marcus Cecil *Précis Writer* 29 Jan.–10 Oct. 1822 (FO 366/381).

Hill, Clement Lloyd *Third Class Junior Clerk* 3 Sept. 1867–30 Dec. 1870 (FO 366/676 p. 198; FO 366/257–8). *Second Class Junior Clerk* 30 Dec. 1870 (*FOL* (Jan. 1872), 5).

Hinchliffe, John *Clerk* 16 July 1782–5 Jan. 1799 (FO 366/669, pt. ii, p. 5). Ret. 5 Jan. 1799 (FO 366/671 pp. 93–6; FO 366/380).

Hole, John Boger *Assistant Junior Clerk* 21 Aug. 1841–9 March 1844 (FO 366/394, 16 Aug. 1841; FO 366/382–3). *Junior Clerk* 9 March 1844–18 Nov. 1851 (FO 366/383). *Second Class Clerk* 18 Nov. 1851–1 April 1857 (FO 366/383–4). *Assistant Clerk* 1 April 1857–4 June 1865 (*FOL* (July 1857), 9). *Senior Clerk* 4 June 1865 (*FOL* (Jan. 1866), 9).

Hope Johnstone, John *Assistant Junior Clerk* 26 June 1846–8 May 1848 (FO 366/674 p. 436; FO 366/383). Res. 8 May 1848 (FO 366/674 p. 465; FO 366/383).

Hoppner, Richard Belgrave *Clerk* 1 Feb. 1801–5 July 1814 (FO 366/671 p. 160).

Salary ceased 5 July 1814 (FO 366/380); app. Consul General, Venice 4 Oct. 1814 (FO 366/247 f. 87).

Howard, Hon. James Kenneth *Précis Writer* 27 April 1835–5 Jan. 1840 (FO 366/673 p. 282; FO 366/382). *Private Secretary to Secretary of State* (Palmerston) 5 Jan. 1840–24 Aug. 1841 (FO 366/382).

Howard, Hon. Kenneth *Third Class Junior Clerk* 20 June 1865–8 June 1868 (FO 366/676 p. 52; FO 366/385). *Second Class Junior Clerk* 8 June 1868 (*FOL* (Jan. 1869), 5).

Howard de Walden, Charles Augustus (Ellis) 6th Lord *Précis Writer* 10 Oct. 1822–26 May 1824 (FO 366/672 p. 307; FO 366/381). *Under Secretary* 26 May 1824–30 May 1828 (FO 366/672 p. 382; FO 366/381).

Acting Under Secretary 24 April–26 May 1824 (FO 366/672 p. 376).

Howick, Charles (Grey) *styled* Viscount *Secretary of State* 24 Sept. 1806–25 March 1807 (FO 366/380; *London Gazette* no. 15960).

Hughes, Loftus William Henry *Third Class Junior Clerk* 15 March 1862–1 Dec. 1866 (FO 366/675 p. 389; FO 366/384–5). *Second Class Junior Clerk* 1 Dec. 1866–29 Dec. 1870 (*FOL* (Jan. 1867), 7). Res. 29 Dec. 1870 (FO 366/258; *FOL* (Jan. 1871), 118).

Huskisson, William Milbanke *Assistant Junior Clerk* 17 Nov. 1834–5 July 1839 (FO 366/673 p. 248; FO 366/382). *Junior Clerk* 5 July 1839–11 April 1843 (FO 366/382–3). *Second Class Clerk* 11 April 1843–13 Jan. 1849 (FO 366/674 pp. 196–7; FO 366/383). D. 13 Jan. 1849 (FO 366/383).

Huttner, John Christian *Translator* 11 Jan. 1809–24 May 1847 (FO 366/671 pp. 362–3). D. 24 May 1847 (*Gent. Mag.* (1847), cxxi (2), 99).

Irving, Francis *Temporary Clerk* (*Librarian's Dept.*) 7 May 1845–1 July 1854 (FO 366/674 p. 384). *Clerk* (*Librarian's Dept.*) 1 July 1854 (FO 366/449 pp. 353–4).

Jackson, Francis James *Clerk* 12 Jan. 1787–*c.* July 1789 (FO 366/669, pt. ii, p. 161). Probably left office 15 July 1789 on app. as Secretary of Legation, Berlin (*Dip. Rep.*, 96).

Jackson, John *Extra Clerk* 5 April 1799–27 Jan. 1806 (FO 366/1292, payment 5 July 1799). *Supernumerary Clerk* 27 Jan. 1806–5 Jan. 1809 (FO 366/671 pp. 284, 301). *Clerk* 5 Jan. 1809–28 March 1822 (FO 366/380). *Second Class Clerk* 28 March 1822–5 July 1830 (PC 2/204 p. 86; FO 366/381–2). Ret. 5 July 1830 (FO 366/673 pp. 122–3, 134–5; FO 366/382).

Jenkins, John Warham *Clerk* 27 March 1782–10 Oct. 1794 (FO 366/669, pt. i, p. 65). Ret. 10 Oct. 1794 (FO 366/427 pp. 108–9; FO 366/1292, payment 27 Feb. 1795).

Jenkinson, Hon. Charles Cecil Cope *Précis Writer* 5 April 1803–5 April 1804 (FO 366/380).

Jervoise *see* **Clarke Jervoise**

Johnson, Henry *Assistant Doorkeeper* 21 Oct. 1861–17 Jan. 1862 (FO 366/675 p. 374). *Office Keeper* 17 Jan. 1862–30 July 1863 (ibid. p. 392). Left office 30 July 1863 on app. as Queen's Home Service Messenger (ibid. p. 475; FO 366/384).

Johnson, William *Clerk* (*Slave Trade Dept.*) 26 Jan. 1837–12 Feb. 1838 (FO 84/261 f. 39). Left office 12 Feb. 1838 on removal to the Commissariat (ibid. ff. 86, 214–15; FO 366/673 p. 349).

Johnstone *see* **Hope Johnstone**

Kennedy, Charles Malcolm *Assistant Junior Clerk* 17 Dec. 1852–1 July 1854 (FO

366/449 p. 61; FO 366/383–4). *Junior Clerk* 1 July 1854–1 April 1857 (*FOL* (Aug. 1854), 9). *First Class Junior Clerk* 1 April 1857–2 Aug. 1863 (*FOL* (July 1857), 9). *Assistant Clerk* 2 Aug. 1863 (*FOL* (Jan. 1864), 9).

Kettle, Henry *Assistant Doorkeeper* 27 Aug. 1827–*c.* 27 Dec. 1841 (FO 366/673 p. 67). Left office by 27 Dec. 1841 (app. of J. Catchpole).

Kingsbury, James *Lamplighter and Coal Porter* 6 May 1817–*c.* 7 July 1840 (FO 366/1292, payment 5 July 1817). Left office by 7 July 1840 (app. of T. Moore).

Lamb, Thomas Davis *Private Secretary to Secretary of State* (Hawkesbury) 20 Feb. 1801–5 July 1802 (FO 366/380).

Langcake, Mary *Housekeeper* 26 Nov. 1863 (FO 366/675 p. 504).

Langley, Henry Fitzroy James *Third Class Junior Clerk* 11 Feb. 1867–30 June 1870 (FO 366/676 p. 149; FO 366/257–8). *Second Class Junior Clerk* 30 June 1870 (*FOL* (Jan. 1871), 5).

Layard, Austen Henry *Parliamentary Under Secretary* 12 Feb.–6 March 1852 (FO 366/449 p. 1; FO 366/383); 15 Aug. 1861–5 July 1866 (FO 366/675 p. 363; FO 366/384–5).

Lee, Henry Austin *Third Class Junior Clerk* 3 Dec. 1870 (FO 366/677 p. 30; FO 366/258).

Leeds, Duke of *see* **Carmarthen,** Marquess of

Le Mesurier, John James *Clerk* (*Slave Trade Dept.*) 19 April 1827–6 March 1834 (FO 96/28/1 ff. 3–4). D. 6 March 1834 (FO 84/162 ff. 155–6).

Lennox *see* **Gordon Lennox**

Lenox Conyngham, George *Supernumerary Clerk* 10 Nov. 1812–5 July 1817 (FO 366/672 p. 47; FO 366/1292, payment 9 Nov. 1812). *Clerk* 5 July 1817–28 March 1822 (FO 366/380). *Junior Clerk* 28 March–29 May 1822 (PC 2/204 p. 86; FO 366/381). *Supernumerary Second Class Clerk* 29 May 1822–5 Jan. 1824 (FO 366/672 p. 267; FO 366/381). *Second Class Clerk* 5 Jan. 1824–16 May 1834 (FO 366/381–2). *Senior Clerk* 16 May 1834–27 July 1841 (FO 366/382). *Chief Clerk* 27 July 1841–26 Nov. 1866 (FO 366/674 pp. 3–4). D. 26 Nov. 1866 (*FOL* (Jan. 1867), 180).

Assistant Précis Writer 5 Jan. 1817–5 July 1819 (FO 366/672 pp. 88, 176). *Clerk Assistant to Under Secretaries* 5 July 1824–5 July 1834 (FO 366/672 p. 394; FO 366/381–2). *Superintendent of Treaty Dept.* 5 July 1834–5 April 1841 (FO 366/673 pp. 261–3; FO 366/382).

Leveson, Granville George (Leveson Gower) *styled* Lord (succ. as 2nd Earl **Granville** 8 Jan. 1846) *Parliamentary Under Secretary* 7 March 1840–3 Sept. 1841 (FO 366/673 pp. 466–7; FO 366/382). *Secretary of State* 26 Dec. 1851–27 Feb. 1852 (*Times*, 27 Dec. 1851; *London Gazette* no. 21277); 6 July 1870 (*Times*, 7 July 1870).

Leveson Gower, Hon. Edward Frederick *Précis Writer* 30 Dec. 1851–27 Feb. 1852 (FO 366/674 p. 531; FO 366/383).

Liddell, Hon. Thomas *Supernumerary Clerk* 13 Feb.–5 April 1824 (FO 366/672 pp. 361–2; FO 366/381). *Junior Clerk* 5 April 1824–5 Jan. 1826 (FO 366/381). Salary ceased 5 Jan. 1826 (ibid.). *Assistant Private Secretary to Secretary of State* (Canning, Dudley) 1 Nov. 1826–5 July 1827 (FO 366/673 p. 30; FO 366/1292, payments 20 June, 5 July 1827).

Lister, Thomas Villiers *Assistant Private Secretary to Secretary of State* (Clarendon) 22 Feb.–23 Aug. 1853 (*FOL* (Jan. 1854), 41). *Assistant Junior Clerk* 23 Aug. 1853–1 July 1854 (FO 366/449 p. 83; FO 366/383–4). *Junior Clerk* 1 July 1854–1

April 1857 (*FOL* (Aug. 1854), 9). *First Class Junior Clerk* 1 April 1857–1 Oct. 1863 (*FOL* (July 1857), 9). *Assistant Clerk* 1 Oct. 1863 (*FOL* (Jan. 1864), 9).

Private Secretary to Secretary of State (Clarendon) 7 Dec. 1857–25 Feb. 1858 (FO 366/449 p. 550; FO 366/384); 3 Nov. 1865–5 July 1866 (FO 366/676 p. 77; FO 366/385); reapp. 10 Dec. 1868 (FO 366/676 p. 369); pd. to 5 July 1870 (FO 366/258). *Précis Writer* 18 June 1859–2 Nov. 1865 (FO 366/675 p. 170; FO 366/384–5).

Londonderry, Marquess of *see* **Castlereagh,** Viscount

Lowry Corry, Armar Henry *Third Class Junior Clerk* 14 May 1857–28 July 1859 (FO 366/449 p. 515; FO 366/384). *Second Class Junior Clerk* 28 July 1859–1 Jan. 1868 (*FOL* (July 1859), 9). *First Class Junior Clerk* 1 Jan. 1868 (*FOL* (March 1868), 7).

Lowth, George *Assistant Junior Clerk* 5 Jan. 1826–5 July 1827 (FO 366/672 p. 443; FO 366/381). *Junior Clerk* 5 July 1827–5 April 1838 (FO 366/673 p. 64; FO 366/381–2). Ret. 5 April 1838 (FO 366/673 pp. 359–61; FO 366/382).

Lumley, John Savile *Temporary Clerk* (*Librarian's Dept.*) 24 Aug. 1841–5 July 1842 (FO 366/674 p. 35). Left office 5 July 1842 on app. as Unpaid Attaché, Berlin (FO 366/228, account for year ending 31 March 1843; *FOL* (1853), 39).

McCarthy, Daniel *Clerk* (*Chief Clerk's Dept.*) 25 May 1868 (FO 366/676 p. 269).

McMahon, Edward *Supernumerary Clerk* 4 July 1818–10 Oct. 1823 (FO 366/672 p. 163; FO 366/1292, payment 3 Nov. 1818). *Junior Clerk* 10 Oct. 1823–5 Jan. 1826 (FO 366/381). *Second Class Clerk* 5 Jan. 1826–5 Jan. 1846 (FO 366/381–3). Ret. 5 Jan. 1846 (FO 366/674 pp. 411–13, 424; FO 366/383).

Maddison, George *Under Secretary* 16 July 1782–2 April 1783 (FO 366/669, pt. ii, p. 5).

Mahon, Philip Henry (Stanhope) *styled* Viscount *Parliamentary Under Secretary* 15 Dec. 1834–17 April 1835 (FO 366/673 p. 256; FO 366/382).

Mallet, Ann Jane *Housekeeper* 5 Jan. 1805–5 July 1806 (FO 366/380). Left office 5 July 1806 (ibid.; FO 366/671 p. 304).

Malmesbury, James Howard (Harris) 3rd Earl of *Secretary of State* 27 Feb.–28 Dec. 1852 (*Times*, 28 Feb. 1852; *London Gazette* no. 21296); 26 Feb. 1858–18 June 1859 (*Times*, 27 Feb. 1858; *London Gazette* no. 22103).

Manby, James *Clerk* 27 March 1782–4 Aug. 1786 (FO 366/669, pt. i, p. 65). D. 4 Aug. 1786 (*Gent. Mag.* (1786), lvi (2), 715).

Mann, Henry *Temporary Clerk* (*Librarian's Dept.*) 24 Aug. 1841–12 Dec. 1844 (FO 366/674 p. 35). Left office 12 Dec. 1844 on app. as Second Paid Attaché, Mission to Persia (ibid. p. 370; FO 366/228, account for year ending 31 March 1845).

March, George Edward *Clerk* (*Librarian's Dept.*) 25 April 1855–19 Nov. 1860 (FO 366/449 p. 392). *Clerk* (*Treaty Dept.*) 19 Nov. 1860 (FO 366/675 p. 289).

Marshall, Samuel Gregory *Supernumerary Clerk* 10 Nov. 1812–5 July 1814 (FO 366/672 p. 47; FO 366/1292, payment 9 Nov. 1812). Salary ceased 5 July 1814 (FO 366/1292, payment 5 July 1814); app. Consul, Emden 3 Sept. 1814 (FO 366/247 f. 33).

Mason, George *Messenger* (*Librarian's Dept.*) 21 April 1857 (FO 366/449 p. 521).

Masterton, Charles *Assistant Translator* 27 Oct. 1823–5 April 1831 (FO 366/672 p. 338). Office abolished 5 April 1831 (FO 366/673 pp. 167, 173).

Maulden, George *Assistant Doorkeeper* 9 Oct. 1849–31 Dec. 1854 (FO 366/674 p. 477). Res. 31 Dec. 1854 (FO 366/449 p. 377; FO 366/384).

Maynard, Reuben John *Assistant Doorkeeper* 9 April 1868 (FO 366/676 p. 265).

Meade, Hon. Robert Henry *Third Class Junior Clerk* 1 June 1859–1 Oct. 1863 (FO 366/675 p. 139; FO 366/384). *Second Class Junior Clerk* 1 Oct. 1863–30 June 1870 (*FOL* (Jan. 1864), 9). *First Class Junior Clerk* 30 June 1870 (*FOL* (Jan. 1871), 5).

Private Secretary to Secretary of State (Granville) 6 July 1870 (FO 366/677 p. 23).

Mellish, Richard Charles *Supernumerary Clerk* 13 Feb.–5 April 1824 (FO 366/672 pp. 361–2; FO 366/381). *Junior Clerk* 5 April 1824–5 July 1827 (FO 366/381). *Second Class Clerk* 5 July 1827–21 Aug. 1841 (FO 366/673 p. 64; FO 366/381–2). *Senior Clerk* 21 Aug. 1841–31 Dec. 1854 (FO 366/382–4). Ret. 31 Dec. 1854 (FO 366/449 pp. 362–5, 371–6; FO 366/384).

Clerk Assistant to Under Secretaries 5 July 1831–21 Aug. 1841 (FO 366/382).

Mesurier *see* **Le Mesurier**

Milbanke, John Ralph *Supernumerary Clerk* 12 Nov. 1823–5 Jan. 1824 (FO 366/672 p. 341; FO 366/381). *Junior Clerk* 5 Jan. 1824–5 July 1826 (FO 366/381). Left office 5 July 1826 on app. as Secretary of Legation, Frankfort (ibid.; *Dip. Rep.*, 57).

Mildmay, Hugo Cornwall St. John *Supernumerary Clerk* 13 Feb.–5 April 1824 (FO 366/672 pp. 361–2; FO 366/381). *Junior Clerk* 5 April 1824–5 July 1830 (FO 366/381–2). *Second Class Clerk* 5 July 1830–8 March 1844 (FO 366/382–3). Left office 8 March 1844 (FO 366/383).

Mills, Thomas *Second Office Porter* 26 July 1851 (FO 366/674 p. 497).

Mitford, Algernon Bertram *Third Class Junior Clerk* 29 Jan. 1859–1 Jan. 1862 (FO 366/675 p. 60; FO 366/384). *Second Class Junior Clerk* 1 Jan. 1862–6 March 1868 (*FOL* (Jan. 1862), 9). Left office 6 March 1868 on app. as Second Secretary, Yeddo (FO 366/385; *FOL* (Jan. 1869), 29, 136).

Molyneux, Hon. Francis George *Assistant Junior Clerk* 31 Aug. 1827–16 May 1834 (FO 366/673 p. 61; FO 366/381–2). *Junior Clerk* 16 May 1834–10 Oct. 1835 (FO 366/382). Left office 10 Oct. 1835 on app. as Secretary of Legation, Frankfort (ibid.; FO 366/673 p. 290; *Dip. Rep.*, 59; FO 366/329 f. 95).

Money, William *Clerk* 27 March 1782–10 Oct. 1793 (FO 366/669, pt. i, p. 65). Ret. 10 Oct. 1793 (FO 366/427 p. 107; FO 366/1292, payment 21 Nov. 1794).

Moore, Francis *Clerk* 5 July 1784–5 Jan. 1803 (FO 366/669, pt. ii, p. 87). Ret. 5 Jan. 1803 (FO 366/671 pp. 225–7; FO 366/380).

Moore, Thomas *Lamplighter and Coal Porter* 7 July 1840–*c.* 15 Oct. 1852 (FO 366/673 p. 483). Left office by 15 Oct. 1852 (app. of Farmer).

Morier, Greville *Assistant Junior Clerk* 26 Aug. 1843–6 Jan. 1846 (FO 366/674 p. 237; FO 366/383). *Junior Clerk* 6 Jan. 1846–16 Dec. 1852 (FO 366/383). *Second Class Clerk* 16 Dec. 1852–1 April 1857 (*FOL* (1853), 9). *Assistant Clerk* 1 April 1857–1 Jan. 1860 (*FOL* (July 1857), 9). *Senior Clerk* 1 Jan. 1860–31 Dec. 1867 (*FOL* (Jan. 1860), 9). Ret. 31 Dec. 1867 (FO 366/676 pp. 241–2, 248–50; FO 366/385).

Mount Charles, Earl of *see* **Conyngham,** Lord Francis Nathaniel

Mulgrave, Henry (Phipps) 3rd Lord *Secretary of State* 11 Jan. 1805–7 Feb. 1806 (*London Gazette* no. 15770; FO 366/380).

Munton, Abel *Office Keeper* 5 Jan. 1812–5 Jan. 1825 (FO 366/672 p. 24). Ret. 5 Jan. 1825 (ibid. pp. 398–9; FO 366/381).

Murray, James *Assistant Junior Clerk* 11 Nov. 1826–5 July 1830 (FO 366/673 p.

47; FO 366/381–2). *Junior Clerk* 5 July 1830–5 July 1839 (FO 366/382). *Second Class Clerk* 5 July 1839–1 Oct. 1851 (FO 366/382–3). *Senior Clerk* 1 Oct. 1851–3 Oct. 1858 (FO 366/383–4). *Assistant Under Secretary* 3 Oct. 1858–3 July 1869 (FO 366/675 pp. 36–9). Ret. 3 July 1869 (FO 366/676 pp. 438–40, 473–4; FO 366/257).

Neale, Henry St. John *Temporary Clerk* (*Librarian's Dept.*) 1 July 1868 (FO 366/676 pp. 267, 340–5).

Newman, Edward Braxton *Extra Clerk* (*Chief Clerk's Dept.*) 20 June 1859–17 April 1865 (FO 366/675 p. 144). *Clerk* (*Chief Clerk's Dept.*) 17 April 1865 (FO 366/676 pp. 49–50).

Nicolson, Arthur *Third Class Junior Clerk* 23 Aug. 1870 (FO 366/677 p. 19; FO 366/258).

Noel, Charles Noel *Clerk* 5 July 1798–5 April 1799 (FO 366/671 pp. 64–5; FO 366/380). Left office 5 April 1799 (FO 366/380).

Norris, Edwin *Translator* 28 Nov. 1847–31 March 1866 (FO 366/674 pp. 459–60). Ret. 31 March 1866 (FO 366/676 pp. 98–9; FO 366/385).

Northcote, Henry Stafford *Third Class Junior Clerk* 18 March 1868 (FO 366/676 p. 234; FO 366/257–8).

Oakes, Augustus Henry *Clerk* (*Librarian's Dept.*) 5 April 1858 (FO 366/675 p. 16).

Oom, Adolphus Kent *Assistant Junior Clerk* 30 April 1824–5 April 1826 (FO 366/672 pp. 377–8; FO 366/381). *Junior Clerk* 5 April 1826–5 April 1839 (FO 366/381–2). *Second Class Clerk* 5 April 1839–13 Dec. 1845 (FO 366/382–3). *Senior Clerk* 13 Dec. 1845–31 March 1859 (FO 366/383–4). Ret. 31 March 1859 (FO 366/675 pp. 122–3, 130–1; FO 366/384).

Otway, Arthur John *Parliamentary Under Secretary* 12 Dec. 1868 (FO 366/676 pp. 371–2).

Owen, William *Assistant Junior Clerk* 22 Dec. 1854–1 April 1857 (FO 366/449 p. 366; FO 366/384). *Second Class Junior Clerk* 1 April 1857–1 Jan. 1862 (*FOL* (July 1857), 9). *First Class Junior Clerk* 1 Jan. 1862 (*FOL* (Jan. 1862), 9).

Paget, Augustus Berkeley *Extra Clerk* 17 March 1840–21 Aug. 1841 (FO 366/673 p. 435). *Assistant Junior Clerk* 21 Aug. 1841–11 April 1843 (FO 366/382–3). *Junior Clerk* 11 April 1843–25 June 1846 (FO 366/674 pp. 196–7; FO 366/383). Left office 25 June 1846 on app. as Second Paid Attaché, Paris (FO 366/383; FO 366/505, 26 June 1846).

Précis Writer 5 Feb.–5 July 1846 (FO 366/674 p. 421; FO 366/383).

Palmerston, Henry John (Temple) 3rd Viscount *Secretary of State* 22 Nov. 1830–17 Nov. 1834 (*Times*, 23 Nov. 1830; *London Gazette* no. 18748); 18 April 1835–3 Sept. 1841 (*Times*, 20 April 1835; *London Gazette* no. 19261); 6 July 1846–26 Dec. 1851 (*Times*, 7 July 1846; *London Gazette* no. 20620).

Parish, Woodbine *Supernumerary Clerk* 15 Aug. 1817–5 July 1818 (FO 366/672 p. 146; FO 366/1292, payment 4 April 1818). *Clerk* 5 July 1818–28 March 1822 (FO 366/380). *Junior Clerk* 28 March 1822–10 Oct. 1823 (PC 2/204 p. 86; FO 366/381). Left office 10 Oct. 1823 on app. as Consul General, Buenos Aires (FO 366/381; FO 83/1219 pp. 287–8).

Clerk Assistant to Under Secretaries 28 March 1822–10 Oct. 1823 (PC 2/204 p. 86; FO 366/381).

Parnther, Charles Henry *Clerk* (*Slave Trade Dept.*) 27 April 1835–*c.* 26 Jan. 1837 (FO 84/184 ff. 33, 35). Left office by 26 Jan. 1837 (FO 84/261 f. 39). Reapp. 5 Feb. 1840 (FO 84/342 f. 30). Dis. 10 Sept. 1853 (FO 366/449 pp. 85–7, 107–8).

Passmore, Udny *Supernumerary Clerk* 15 Aug. 1817–10 Oct. 1823 (FO 366/672 p. 146; FO 366/1292, payment 10 Oct. 1817). Salary ceased 10 Oct. 1823 on app. as Vice Consul, Peru (FO 366/381; FO 366/672 pp. 344–5).

Pearl, Albert Charles *Office Keeper* 24 Aug. 1869 (FO 366/676 p. 431).

Pennell, John Croker *Assistant Junior Clerk* 9 March 1844–26 June 1846 (FO 366/674 p. 262; FO 366/383). *Junior Clerk* 26 June 1846–1 July 1854 (FO 366/383–4). *Second Class Clerk* 1 July 1854–1 April 1857 (*FOL* (Aug. 1854), 9). *Assistant Clerk* 1 April 1857–2 Aug. 1863 (*FOL* (July 1857), 9). *Senior Clerk* 2 Aug. 1863–3 June 1865 (*FOL* (Jan. 1864), 9). D. 3 June 1865 (*FOL* (July 1865), 168).

Pettingal, Charles *Clerk* (*Slave Trade Dept.*) 22 Nov. 1825–10 Oct. 1843 (FO 96/28/1 ff. 3–4). Left office 10 Oct. 1843 on app. as Arbitrator, Anglo-Portuguese Commission for Suppression of Slave Trade, Boa Vista, Cape Verde Islands (FO 366/383; FO 83/892 pp. 243–50).

Pierrepont, Hon. Henry Manvers *Private Secretary to Secretary of State* (Hawkesbury) pd. from 5 July 1802 to 5 July 1803 (FO 366/380); probably remained in office without salary after undertaking mission to Sweden July 1803 until May 1804 when Hawkesbury ceased to be Secretary of State (ibid.; *Royal Kal.* (1804), 132).

Planta, Joseph *Supernumerary Clerk* 27 Sept. 1802–5 Jan. 1803 (FO 366/671 p. 218). *Clerk* 5 Jan. 1803–5 July 1817 (FO 366/380). *Under Secretary* 5 July 1817–19 April 1827 (FO 366/672 p. 144; FO 366/380–1).

Assistant Précis Writer 5 July–10 Oct. 1807 (FO 366/380). *Précis Writer* 5 Jan. 1809–5 July 1817 (ibid.).

Private Secretary to Secretary of State (Castlereagh) 5 July 1814–5 July 1817 (ibid.).

Plasket, Edward *Clerk* (*Consular Dept.*) 30 Aug. 1861–1 April 1868 (FO 366/675 p. 364). *Clerk* (*Chief Clerk's Dept.*) 1 April 1868 (FO 366/676 pp. 270–1).

Pleydell Bouverie, Hon. Edward *Précis Writer* 5 Jan.–20 April 1840 (FO 366/382; FO 366/673 p. 483).

Ponsonby, John George Brabazon (*styled* Hon. 19 July 1834) *Précis Writer* 3 May 1833–17 Nov. 1834 (FO 366/673 p. 227; FO 366/382).

Ponsonby, Hon. Spencer Cecil Brabazon *Extra Clerk* 29 Oct. 1840–21 Aug. 1841 (FO 366/673 p. 505). *Assistant Junior Clerk* 21 Aug. 1841–7 Aug. 1843 (FO 366/382–3). *Junior Clerk* 7 Aug. 1843–1 Oct. 1851 (FO 366/383). *Second Class Clerk* 1 Oct. 1851–1 April 1857 (FO 366/383–4). *Assistant Clerk* 1 April–6 Dec. 1857 (*FOL* (July 1857), 9). Left office 6 Dec. 1857 on app. as Controller of Accounts, Lord Chamberlain's Dept. (FO 366/384; W. A. Lindsay, *The Royal Household* (London 1898), 159).

Private Secretary to Secretary of State (Palmerston, Granville) 9 July 1846–27 Feb. 1852 (FO 366/674 p. 439; FO 366/383); (Clarendon) 22 Feb. 1853–6 Dec. 1857 (FO 366/383–4).

Precious, William *Office Keeper* probably app. 1790 in place of Schaw (*Royal Kal.* (1790), 104). Left office 10 Oct. 1795 (FO 366/380).

Quick, William Fortescue *Clerk* (*Librarian's Dept.*) 24 Aug. 1841–19 Aug. 1844 (FO 366/674 p. 35). D. 19 Aug. 1844 (FO 366/383).

Reed, John *Office Keeper* 24 Nov. 1824–5 July 1825 (FO 366/1292, payment 8 Jan. 1825). Left office 5 July 1825 (ibid., payments 6 July, 29 Oct. 1825).

Rice *see* **Spring Rice**

Rich, Henry Osborn Ludlow *Temporary Clerk* (*Librarian's Dept.*) 24 Aug. 1841–

15 April 1845 (FO 366/674 p. 35). Left office 15 April 1845 (FO 366/228, account for year ending 31 March 1846).

Robertson, Charles Boyd *Third Class Junior Clerk* 30 Jan. 1865–7 March 1868 (FO 366/675 p. 542; FO 366/385). *Second Class Junior Clerk* 7 March 1868 (*FOL* (Jan. 1869), 5).

Robertson, Duncan *Clerk* (*Librarian's Dept.*) 29 Jan. 1861 (FO 366/675 p. 296).

Robinson, Henry Stirling *Assistant Junior Clerk* 20 Sept. 1826–27 Aug. 1829 (FO 366/673 pp. 14–16; FO 366/381–2). Left office 27 Aug. 1829 (FO 366/382).

Rolfe, Robert *Office Keeper* 31 Jan. 1857 (FO 366/449 p. 489).

Rolleston, Henry John *Supernumerary Clerk* 1 Feb. 1801–17 Feb. 1802 (FO 366/671 p. 160). *Clerk* 17 Feb. 1802–28 March 1822 (ibid. p. 203; FO 366/380). *Second Class Clerk* 28 March 1822–5 Jan. 1824 (PC 2/204 p. 86; FO 366/381). *Senior Clerk* 5 Jan. 1824–16 May 1834 (FO 366/381–2). D. 16 May 1834 (FO 366/382).

Superintendent of Treaty Dept. 5 April 1813–16 May 1834 (FO 366/672 pp. 68–70; FO 366/380–2).

Rolleston, Stephen *Clerk* 31 July 1783–10 Aug. 1804 (FO 366/669, pt. ii, p. 47). *Second Chief Clerk* 10 Aug. 1804–28 Sept. 1817 (FO 366/671 pp. 298–300; FO 366/380). *Chief Clerk* 28 Sept. 1817–5 Jan. 1824 (FO 366/380–1). Ret. 5 Jan. 1824 (FO 366/672 pp. 346–8; FO 366/381).

Assistant to Under Secretaries 20 Feb. 1801–5 Jan. 1824 (FO 366/671 pp. 186–8; FO 366/380–1).

Romer, Arthur *Temporary Clerk* (*Librarian's Dept.*) 1 July 1868–16 March 1870 (FO 366/676 pp. 267, 340–5). Dis. 16 March 1870 (FO 366/677 pp. 1–7).

Ross, James Tyrell *Private Secretary to Secretary of State* (Canning) 5 April 1807–10 Oct. 1809 (FO 366/380).

Russell, Arthur John Edward *Private Secretary to Secretary of State* (Russell) 29 Dec. 1852–21 Feb. 1853 (FO 366/449 p. 65; FO 366/383).

Russell, George *Assistant Private Secretary to Secretary of State* (Russell) 19 June 1859–Oct. 1865 (*FOL* (Jan. 1866), 148).

Russell, Lord John (cr. Earl **Russell** 30 July 1861) *Secretary of State* 28 Dec. 1852–21 Feb. 1853 (*Times*, 29 Dec. 1852; *London Gazette* no. 21396); 18 June 1859–3 Nov. 1865 (*Times*, 20 June 1859; *London Gazette* no. 22276).

Russell, Odo William Leopold *Assistant Under Secretary* 10 Aug. 1870 (FO 366/677 p. 23).

Russell, Reginald *Third Class Junior Clerk* 22 Feb. 1858–1 Jan. 1860 (FO 366/675 p. 8; FO 366/384). *Second Class Junior Clerk* 1 Jan. 1860–1 June 1867 (*FOL* (Jan. 1860), 9). Res. 1 June 1867 (FO 366/676 p. 199; FO 366/385).

Ryder, Hon. Dudley (succ. as 2nd Lord **Harrowby** 20 June 1803) *Under Secretary* 24 Aug. 1789–20 Feb. 1790 (FO 366/669, pt. ii, p. 238; FO 366/670 p. 16). *Secretary of State* 12 May 1804–11 Jan. 1805 (FO 366/380; *London Gazette* no. 15701).

Ryder, Hon. Frederick Dudley *Assistant Junior Clerk* 23 April 1827–29 Oct. 1834 (FO 366/673 pp. 34–5; FO 366/381–2). Dis. 29 Oct. 1834 (FO 366/673 pp. 237–8; FO 366/382).

St. John, Hon. St. Andrew *Under Secretary* 2 April–19 Dec. 1783 (FO 366/669, pt. ii, p. 36).

Samways, James *Office Keeper* 3 March–2 Aug. 1838 (FO 366/673 p. 348). Left office 2 Aug. 1838 on app. as Messenger to First Lord of Treasury (ibid. p. 365; *Treasury Officials 1660–1870*, comp. J. C. Sainty (London 1972), 148).

Sanders, Henry William *Extra Clerk* (*Chief Clerk's Dept.*) 17 April 1826–5 June 1859 (FO 366/1292, payment 22 July 1826). Res. 5 June 1859 (FO 366/675 pp. 142–3).

Sanderson, Thomas Henry *Third Class Junior Clerk* 23 April 1859–2 Aug. 1863 (FO 366/675 p. 70; FO 366/384). *Second Class Junior Clerk* 2 Aug. 1863–3 July 1869 (*FOL* (Jan. 1864), 9). *First Class Junior Clerk* 3 July 1869 (*FOL* (Jan. 1870), 5).

Private Secretary: *to Parliamentary Under Secretary* (Layard) 1 Feb.–5 July 1866 (FO 366/676 p. 94; FO 366/385); *to Secretary of State* (Stanley) 6 July 1866–9 Dec. 1868 (FO 366/676 p. 112; FO 366/385).

Sasse, Frederick Richard *Clerk* (*Librarian's Dept.*) 10 Nov. 1844–3 Dec. 1857 (FO 366/674 p. 368). *Probationary Sub-Librarian* 3 Dec. 1857–17 Jan. 1859 (FO 366/449 p. 549). *Clerk* (*Librarian's Dept.*) 17 Jan. 1859 (FO 366/675 p. 55).

Saunders, Sidney Smith *Clerk* (*Consular Dept.*) 5 July 1826–18 April 1835 (FO 366/673 p. 19). Left office 18 April 1835 on app. as Consul, Preveza (ibid. p. 279; FO 83/1220 pp. 200–3).

Schaw, John *Office Keeper* March 1782–*c.* 14 July 1790 (*Royal Kal.* (1783), 110; *1st Rept. on Fees*, 32–3). Probably left office 14 July 1790 on app. as King's Messenger (FO 366/670 p. 43).

Scheener, Edward *Supernumerary Clerk* 5 Aug. 1809–5 July 1814 (FO 366/671 pp. 392–3). *Clerk* 5 July 1814–28 March 1822 (FO 366/380). *Junior Clerk* 28 March–29 May 1822 (PC 2/204 p. 86; FO 366/381). *Supernumerary Second Class Clerk* 29 May 1822–10 Oct. 1823 (FO 366/672 p. 267; FO 366/381). *Second Class Clerk* 10 Oct. 1823–5 July 1830 (FO 366/381–2). Ret. 5 July 1830 (FO 366/673 pp. 122–3, 134–5; FO 366/382).

Scott, Charles *Assistant Junior Clerk* 11 Jan. 1828–17 Nov. 1834 (FO 366/673 p. 65; FO 366/381–2). *Junior Clerk* 17 Nov. 1834–5 July 1839 (FO 366/382). *Second Class Clerk* 5 July 1839–28 Oct. 1841 (ibid.). D. 28 Oct. 1841 (ibid.).

Scott, Henry Charles *Clerk* (*Slave Trade Dept.*) 5 Nov. 1842–10 Sept. 1853 (FO 366/674 p. 195). Dis. 10 Sept. 1853 (FO 366/449 pp. 85–7).

Scott, Henry Dundas *Clerk* (*Chief Clerk's Dept.*) 5 July 1814–18 June 1866 (FO 366/1292, payment 10 Oct. 1814). Ret. 18 June 1866 (FO 366/676 p. 108; FO 366/385).

Seale, Robert Bewick *Clerk* (*Librarian's Dept.*) 24 Aug. 1841–23 Oct. 1844 (FO 366/674 p. 35). Dis. 23 Oct. 1844 (ibid. pp. 355–7).

Seymour, George Hamilton *Précis Writer* 5 Jan. 1821–29 Jan. 1822 (FO 366/380). *Private Secretary to Secretary of State* (Londonderry) app. 29 Jan. 1822 (FO 366/381); pd. to 10 Oct. 1822 (ibid.).

Shee, Sir George, 2nd Bart. *Parliamentary Under Secretary* 26 Nov. 1830–12 Nov. 1834 (FO 366/673 p. 151; FO 366/382).

Shelburne, Henry (Petty Fitzmaurice) *styled* Earl of *Parliamentary Under Secretary* 4 July 1856–25 Feb. 1858 (FO 366/449 p. 421; FO 366/384).

Sheridan, Richard Brinsley *Under Secretary* 27 March–16 July 1782 (FO 366/669, pt. i, p. 65).

Skelton, George *Clerk* (*Slave Trade Dept.*) 28 Feb. 1845–30 Nov. 1856 (FO 366/674 p. 383). Left office 30 Nov. 1856 on app. as Arbitrator, International Commission for Suppression of Slave Trade, Sierra Leone (FO 366/384; *FOL* (Jan. 1857), 26, 76).

Smith, Culling Charles *Under Secretary* 13 Dec. 1809–27 Feb. 1812 (FO 366/671 p. 402; FO 366/380).

Smith, George *Private Secretary to Secretary of State* (Mulgrave) probably app. Jan. 1805; pd. from 5 Jan. 1805 to 7 Feb. 1806 (FO 366/380).

Smythe, Hon. George Augustus Frederick Percy Sydney *Parliamentary Under Secretary* 27 Jan.–5 July 1846 (FO 366/674 p. 418; FO 366/383).

Sneyd, Jeremiah *Chief Clerk* 27 March 1782–18 April 1792 (FO 366/669, pt. i, p. 65). Ret. 18 April 1792 (FO 366/670 p. 125).

Southcott, Mary *Housekeeper* March 1782–*c.* Sept. 1783 (*Royal Kal.* (1783), 110). D. between 12 Aug. and 9 Sept. 1783 (Prob. 11/1108 f. 480).

Spring Rice, Hon. Thomas Charles William *Assistant Junior Clerk* 15 Dec. 1839–21 Aug. 1841 (FO 366/673 p. 409; FO 366/382). *Junior Clerk* 21 Aug. 1841–26 June 1846 (FO 366/382–3). *Second Class Clerk* 26 June 1846–13 March 1857 (FO 366/383–4). *Senior Clerk* 13 March 1857–3 July 1869 (*FOL* (July 1857), 9). *Assistant Under Secretary* 3 July 1869–13 July 1870 (FO 366/676 p. 462). D. 13 July 1870 (*FOL* (Jan. 1871), 199).

Superintendent of Commercial and Consular Dept. 1 Oct. 1866–3 July 1869 (FO 366/676 pp. 118–21; FO 366/257).

Spyer, Anthony *Deputy Office Porter* had been in office 'for some time past' on d. Sept. 1802 (FO 366/671 p. 228).

Spyer, Edward *Deputy Office Porter* in office by Sept. 1824 (FO 366/393, Sept. 1824). *Second Office Porter* 6 July 1843–*c.* 26 July 1851 (FO 366/673 p. 238). Left office by 26 July 1851 (app. of Mills).

Stahl, Conrath *Office Keeper* 5 April 1826–5 Jan. 1838 (FO 366/381–2). Ret. 5 Jan. 1838 (FO 366/673 pp. 334–5, 340; FO 366/382).

Stanley, Edward Henry (Stanley) *styled* Lord *Parliamentary Under Secretary* 18 May–28 Dec. 1852 (FO 366/449 pp. 8–9; FO 366/383). *Secretary of State* 6 July 1866–9 Dec. 1868 (*Times*, 7 July 1866; *London Gazette* no. 23134).

Stanley, Hon. Edward John (cr. Lord **Eddisbury** 12 May 1848; succ. as 2nd Lord **Stanley of Alderley** 23 Oct. 1850) *Parliamentary Under Secretary* 6 July 1846–31 Dec. 1851 (FO 366/674 p. 440; FO 366/383).

Stanley, Henry Edward John (*styled* Hon. 12 May 1848) *Assistant Précis Writer* 20 Dec. 1847–*c.* April 1849 (FO 366/674 p. 461; FO 366/383). *Précis Writer c.* April 1849–23 Dec. 1851 (FO 366/383).

Stapleton, Augustus Granville *Supernumerary Clerk* 12 Nov. 1823–5 Jan. 1824 (FO 366/672 p. 341; FO 366/381). *Junior Clerk* 5 Jan. 1824–5 Jan. 1827 (FO 366/381). *Second Class Clerk* 5 Jan.–31 Aug. 1827 (ibid.). Left office 31 Aug. 1827 on app. as Commissioner of Customs (FO 366/673 p. 64; C 66/4325).

Private Secretary to Secretary of State (Canning) 5 April 1824–30 April 1827 (FO 366/381).

Staveley, Thomas *Supernumerary Clerk* 24 Dec. 1814–28 Sept. 1817 (FO 366/672 p. 91; FO 366/1292, payment 5 April 1815). *Clerk* 28 Sept. 1817–28 March 1822 (FO 366/380). *Junior Clerk* 28 March 1822–5 April 1824 (PC 2/204 p. 86; FO 366/381). *Second Class Clerk* 5 April 1824-5 April 1839 (FO 366/381–2). *Senior Clerk* 5 April 1839–12 March 1857 (FO 366/382–4). Ret. 12 March 1857 (FO 366/449 pp. 490–2, 494–5, 511–12; FO 366/384).

Clerk Assistant to Under Secretaries 28 March 1822–21 Aug. 1841 (PC 2/204 p. 86; FO 366/381–2).

Staveley, Thomas George *Assistant Junior Clerk* 26 Aug. 1843–26 June 1846 (FO 366/674 p. 237; FO 366/383). *Junior Clerk* 26 June 1846–10 April 1854 (FO 366/383–4). *Second Class Clerk* 10 April 1854–1 April 1857 (*FOL* (Aug. 1854), 9). *Assistant Clerk* 1 April 1857–22 Aug. 1860 (*FOL* (July 1857), 9). *Senior Clerk* 22 Aug. 1860 (*FOL* (Jan. 1861), 9).

Stephens, Francis Stanley Maxwell *Assistant Junior Clerk* 7 May 1854–1 Dec. 1856 (FO 366/449 p. 164; FO 366/384). *Junior Clerk* 1 Dec. 1856–1 April 1857 (FO 366/384). *Second Class Junior Clerk* 1 April 1857–1 June 1859 (ibid.). *First Class Junior Clerk* 1 June 1859–3 July 1869 (*FOL* (July 1859), 9). *Assistant Clerk* 3 July 1869 (*FOL* (Jan. 1870), 5).

Stepney *see* **Cowell**

Stopford, William Bruce *Assistant Junior Clerk* 5 Jan. 1826–5 Jan. 1828 (FO 366/381). *Junior Clerk* 5 Jan. 1828–5 July 1839 (FO 366/381–2). *Second Class Clerk* 5 July 1839–6 Aug. 1843 (FO 366/382–3). Res. 6 Aug. 1843 (FO 366/674 p. 235; FO 366/383).

Précis Writer 3 Sept. 1841–24 Nov. 1843 (FO 366/674 p. 144; FO 366/382–3).

Strangways *see* **Fox Strangways**

Streatfield, Frederick Henry Thomas *Clerk* (*Librarian's Dept.*) 22 Dec. 1868 (FO 366/676 p. 360).

Stuart *see* **Crichton Stuart**

Sulivan, Stephen Henry *Assistant Junior Clerk* 17 Aug. 1832–17 Nov. 1834 (FO 366/673 p. 217; FO 366/382). Left office 17 Nov. 1834 on app. as Paid Attaché, The Hague (FO 366/382; FO 366/329 f. 118).

Précis Writer 16 Sept. 1832–2 May 1833 (FO 366/673 p. 218; FO 366/382). *Private Secretary to Secretary of State* (Palmerston) 3 May 1833–17 Nov. 1834 (FO 366/673 p. 227; FO 366/382).

Synge, William Webb Follett *Assistant Junior Clerk* 26 June 1846–18 Nov. 1851 (FO 366/674 p. 436; FO 366/383). *Junior Clerk* 18 Nov. 1851–1 July 1854 (FO 366/383–4). *Second Class Clerk* 1 July 1854–1 April 1857 (*FOL* (Aug. 1854), 9). *First Class Junior Clerk* 1 April–7 Dec. 1857 (FO 366/384). *Assistant Clerk* 7 Dec. 1857–31 Dec. 1861 (*FOL* (Jan. 1858), 9). Left office 31 Dec. 1861 on app. as Commissioner and Consul General, Sandwich Islands (FO 366/384; *FOL* (Jan. 1862), 36, 151).

Talbot, James *Office Porter* July 1795–4 July 1843 (FO 366/1292, payment 18 Nov. 1795). D. 4 July 1843 (FO 366/393, 22 Sept. 1843).

Talbot, Robert *Private Secretary to Secretary of State* (Howick) app. 12 Dec. 1806 (FO 366/380); probably left office with Howick 25 March 1807; pd. to 5 April 1807 (ibid.).

Talbot, Thomas *Deputy Office Porter* probably app. 1802; had been in office 23 years on ret. 10 Oct. 1825 (FO 366/673 pp. 17–18, 23).

Taunton, Walter Greene *Temporary Clerk* (*Librarian's Dept.*) 28 Nov. 1844–23 June 1845 (FO 366/674 p. 369). Res. 23 June 1845 on becoming a member of the Stock Exchange (ibid. p. 385).

Taylor, Aucher Cornwall *Clerk* (*Chief Clerk's Dept.*) 18 Aug. 1869 (FO 366/676 p. 470).

Taylor, Bridges *Assistant Junior Clerk* 29 Oct. 1834–5 April 1839 (FO 366/673 p.

239; FO 366/382). *Junior Clerk* 5 April 1839–21 Aug. 1841 (FO 366/382). *Second Class Clerk* 21 Aug. 1841–13 Dec. 1852 (FO 366/382–3). Left office 13 Dec. 1852 on app. as Consul, Elsinore (FO 366/383; *FOL* (1853), 17, 44).
Précis Writer 1 April–14 Dec. 1852 (FO 366/449 p. 10; FO 366/383).

Taylor, Brook *Clerk* 27 Sept. 1793–24 Feb. 1796 (Add. MS 59229 f. 104). *Private Secretary to Secretary of State* (Grenville) 24 Feb. 1796–5 Jan. 1801 (FO 366/670 p. 371; FO 366/380).
Précis Writer 5 Sept. 1798–20 Feb. 1801 (FO 366/671 p. 73; FO 366/380).

Taylor, Brook Pakenham Bridges *Third Class Junior Clerk* 5 Aug. 1868 (FO 366/676 p. 284; FO 366/257–8).

Taylor, Herbert *Clerk* 2 Aug. 1792–*c.* 7 April 1794 (FO 366/670 p. 138). Probably left office 7 April 1794 on app. as Cornet, 2nd Dragoon Guards (*The Taylor Papers*, ed. E. Taylor (London 1913), 45; *London Gazette* no. 13638).

Taylor, William Watkinson *Clerk* 27 Sept. 1793–*c.* 15 July 1797 (Add. MS 59229 f. 104). D. *c.* 15 July 1797 (FO 366/380; *The Taylor Papers*, ed. E. Taylor (London 1913), 51).

Temple, George (Nugent Temple Grenville) 3rd Earl *Secretary of State* 19–23 Dec. 1783 (*London Gazette* no. 12502).

Temple, Hon. William *Précis Writer* 22 Nov. 1830–16 Sept. 1832 (FO 366/382).

Tenterden, Lord *see* **Abbott,** Charles Stuart Aubrey

Townshend, John Villiers Stuart *Extra Clerk* 18 June 1850–1 Oct. 1851 (FO 366/674 p. 496). *Assistant Junior Clerk* 1 Oct. 1851–31 March 1854 (ibid. p. 521; FO 366/383). Res. 31 March 1854 (FO 366/383; FO 366/685).

Trench, Joanna *Housekeeper* 18 May 1814–5 July 1824 (FO 366/380–1). Left office 5 July 1824 (FO 366/381).

Trotter, John Bernard *Private Secretary to Secretary of State* (Fox, Howick) 7 Feb.–12 Dec. 1806 (FO 366/380).
Précis Writer 6 March 1806–5 July 1807 (ibid.).

Turner, Adolphus *Assistant Junior Clerk* 30 April 1824–5 Jan. 1826 (FO 366/672 pp. 377–8; FO 366/381). *Junior Clerk* 5 Jan. 1826–16 May 1834 (FO 366/381–2). *Second Class Clerk* 16 May 1834–11 April 1843 (FO 366/382–3). Left office 11 April 1843 on app. as Chargé d'Affaires and Consul General, Monte Video (FO 366/674 pp. 196–7; *Dip. Rep.*, 191).

Turner, Richard *Office Keeper* March 1782–*c.* 1787 (*Royal Kal.* (1783), 110; *1st Rept. on Fees*, 32). Last occ. 1787 (*Royal Kal.* (1787), 104).

Turner, William *Assistant Private Secretary to Secretary of State* (Canning) 10 Oct. 1808–20 Jan. 1809 (FO 366/671 p. 356; FO 366/1292, payment 9 Jan. 1809). *Clerk* 20 Jan. 1809–28 March 1822 (FO 366/671 p. 367). *Second Class Clerk* 28 March 1822–10 Oct. 1823 (PC 2/204 p. 86; FO 366/381). Left office 10 Oct. 1823 on app. as Secretary to Commission for Settlement of Claims of British and Spanish Subjects (FO 366/381; FO 366/672 pp. 342–3).

Tyler, John *Office Keeper* 2 Aug. 1838–31 Dec. 1861 (FO 366/673 p. 365; FO 366/383–4). Ret. 31 Dec. 1861 (FO 366/675 pp. 393–5; FO 366/384).

Urquhart, Mary *Housekeeper* 5 July 1824–16 March 1836 (FO 366/381–2). D. 16 March 1836 (FO 366/382).

Vaughan, Charles Richard *Private Secretary to Secretary of State* (Bathurst) pd. from 11 Oct. 1809 (FO 366/380); probably left office with Bathurst 6 Dec. 1809; pd. to 5 Jan. 1810 (ibid.).

Venfield, John *Office Keeper* 5 July 1825–11 Dec. 1845 (FO 366/1292, payment 10 Oct. 1825; FO 366/673 p. 236). Ret. 11 Dec. 1845 (FO 366/674 pp. 397–9; FO 366/383).

Vernon, Greville Richard (*styled* Hon. 28 June 1859) *Assistant Junior Clerk* 7 May–1 Oct. 1854 (FO 366/449 p. 165; FO 366/384). *Junior Clerk* 1 Oct. 1854–1 April 1857 (*FOL* (Jan. 1855), 9). *Second Class Junior Clerk* 1 April 1857–1 Jan. 1859 (FO 366/384). *First Class Junior Clerk* 1 Jan.–27 July 1859 (*FOL* (Jan. 1859), 9). Res. 27 July 1859 (FO 366/675 p. 172; FO 366/384).

Vesey Fitzgerald, William Robert Seymour *Parliamentary Under Secretary* 26 Feb. 1858–18 June 1859 (FO 366/675 pp. 8–9; FO 366/384).

Villiers, Hon. Francis Hyde *Third Class Junior Clerk* 30 Dec. 1870 (FO 366/677 p. 30; FO 366/258).

Vincent, Sir Francis, 9th Bart. *Under Secretary* 20 Feb. 1806–30 March 1807 (FO 366/671 pp. 290–1, 319).

Vincent, George *Office Keeper* 20 July 1864 (FO 366/675 p. 524).

Vivian, Hon. Hussey Crespigny *Assistant Junior Clerk* 18 Nov. 1851–10 April 1854 (FO 366/674 p. 521; FO 366/383–4). *Junior Clerk* 10 April 1854–1 Dec. 1856 (*FOL* (Aug. 1854), 9). *Second Class Clerk* 1 Dec. 1856–1 April 1857 (*FOL* (Jan. 1857), 9). *First Class Junior Clerk* 1 April 1857–1 June 1859 (FO 366/384). *Assistant Clerk* 1 June 1859–3 July 1869 (*FOL* (July 1859), 9). *Senior Clerk* 3 July 1869 (*FOL* (Jan. 1870), 5).

Vyner, Reginald Arthur *Third Class Junior Clerk* 16 Aug. 1859–11 Dec. 1860 (FO 366/675 p. 173; FO 366/384). Res. 11 Dec. 1860 (FO 366/384); elected M.P. 22 Dec. 1860 (HC 69–I (1878) lxii, pt. ii, p. 456).

Walmisley, Arthur *Temporary Clerk* (*Librarian's Dept.*) 9 Aug. 1845–1 July 1854 (FO 366/674 p. 386). *Clerk* (*Librarian's Dept.*) 1 July 1854 (FO 366/449 pp. 353–4).

Walpole, Hon. George *Under Secretary* 20 Feb. 1806–30 March 1807 (FO 366/671 pp. 290–1, 319).

Walpole, John *Assistant Office Keeper* 1 Aug. 1793–5 April 1795 (FO 366/1292, payments 24 Jan., 11 Aug. 1795). *Office Keeper* 5 April 1795–22 Jan. 1807 (FO 366/380). Ret. 22 Jan. 1807 (FO 366/671 p. 314).

Walpole, Hon. John *Private Secretary to Secretary of State* (Palmerston) 25 Nov. 1830–5 April 1833 (FO 366/673 pp. 164, 227; FO 366/382).

Walsham, John *Assistant Junior Clerk* 1 Oct. 1854–13 March 1857 (FO 366/449 p. 358; FO 366/384). *Junior Clerk* 13 March–1 April 1857 (FO 366/384). *Second Class Junior Clerk* 1 April 1857–31 Dec. 1859 (ibid.). Left office 31 Dec. 1859 on app. as Paid Attaché, Mexico (ibid.; *FOL* (Jan. 1860), 32, 134).

Warburton, Joseph William *Assistant Junior Clerk* 31 March–1 April 1857 (FO 366/449 p. 488). *Third Class Junior Clerk* 1 April 1857–1 April 1859 (ibid. pp. 500–3; FO 366/384). *Second Class Junior Clerk* 1 April 1859–1 Dec. 1866 (FO 366/384). *First Class Junior Clerk* 1 Dec. 1866 (*FOL* (Jan. 1867), 7).

Ward, Edward Michael *Private Secretary to Secretary of State* (Castlereagh) 10 Oct. 1812–5 July 1814 (FO 366/380).

Ward, Robert *Under Secretary* 25 Jan. 1805–7 Feb. 1806 (FO 366/671 p. 265; FO 366/380).

Ward, Thomas Lawrence *Supernumerary Clerk* 29 Nov. 1817–10 Oct. 1823 (FO 366/672 pp. 148, 150). *Junior Clerk* 10 Oct. 1823–5 April 1824 (FO 366/381). *Second Class Clerk* 5 April 1824–16 Aug. 1841 (FO 366/381–2). *Senior Clerk* 16

Aug. 1841–31 Dec. 1859 (FO 366/394, 16 Aug. 1841; FO 366/382–4). Ret. 31 Dec. 1859 (FO 366/675 pp. 177–9, 183–7; FO 366/384).

Clerk Assistant to Under Secretaries 5 Jan. 1825–5 July 1831 (FO 366/381–2); 5 July 1834–21 Aug. 1841 (FO 366/382).

Warren, Charles *Clerk* 20 Oct. 1790–5 July 1818 (FO 366/670 p. 61). Ret. 5 July 1818 (FO 366/672 pp. 156, 158–9; FO 366/380).

Waterpark, Lord *see* **Cavendish,** Hon. Henry Anson

Watson, Ann *Housekeeper* 18 March 1836–30 Sept. 1863 (FO 366/673 p. 306). Ret. 30 Sept. 1863 (FO 366/675 pp. 491–2, 500–2; FO 366/384).

Weller, Joseph *Doorkeeper* 10 Feb. 1851 (FO 366/674 p. 495).

Wellesley, Richard Colley (Wellesley) 1st Marquess *Secretary of State* 6 Dec. 1809–18 Feb. 1812 (FO 366/380; *London Gazette* no. 16322; FO 366/672 p. 42).

Wellesley, Richard Gerald *Extra Clerk* 10 May–22 Nov. 1839 (FO 366/673 p. 378). *Assistant Junior Clerk* 22 Nov. 1839–21 Aug. 1841 (FO 366/382). *Junior Clerk* 21 Aug. 1841–6 Jan. 1846 (FO 366/382–3). *Second Class Clerk* 6 Jan. 1846–1 Jan. 1856 (FO 366/383–4). *Senior Clerk* 1 Jan. 1856–21 Aug. 1860 (*FOL* (July 1856), 9). Ret. 21 Aug. 1860 (FO 366/675 pp. 266–7, 270–1; FO 366/384).

Wellesley *see also* **Wesley**

Wellington, Arthur (Wellesley) 1st Duke of *Secretary of State* 17 Nov. 1834–18 April 1835 (*Times*, 18 Nov. 1834; *London Gazette* no. 19211).

Werry, James *Lamplighter and Coal Porter* pd. from 5 Jan. 1806 to 10 Oct. 1812 (FO 366/1292, payments 9 May 1806, 10 Oct. 1812).

Wesley (*or* **Wellesley**), Hon. Henry *Précis Writer* 5 April 1795–10 Oct. 1797 (FO 366/380).

Williams Wynn, Henry Watkin *Clerk* 1 April 1799–1 Feb. 1801 (FO 366/671 pp. 117–18). *Private Secretary to Secretary of State* (Grenville) 1–20 Feb. 1801 (ibid. p. 155). *Précis Writer* 20 Feb. 1801–5 April 1803 (FO 366/380).

Wilson, Robert *Temporary Clerk* (*Librarian's Dept.*) 5 April 1826–11 Aug. 1839 (FO 366/673 p. 4). D. 11 Aug. 1839 (FO 366/228, account for year ending 31 March 1840).

Wodehouse, John (Wodehouse) 3rd Lord *Parliamentary Under Secretary* 29 Dec. 1852–25 May 1856 (FO 366/449 pp. 63–4; FO 366/383–4); 20 June 1859–14 Aug. 1861 (FO 366/675 pp. 170–1; FO 366/384).

Wolff, Henry Drummond *Clerk* (*Treaty Dept.*) 17 Oct. 1846–14 Jan. 1849 (FO 366/674 p. 445). *Assistant Junior Clerk* 14 Jan. 1849–16 Dec. 1852 (ibid. pp. 475–6; FO 366/383). *Junior Clerk* 16 Dec. 1852–1 Jan. 1855 (*FOL* (1853), 9). *Second Class Clerk* 1 Jan. 1855–1 April 1857 (*FOL* (June 1855), 9). *First Class Junior Clerk* 1 April 1857–1 April 1859 (FO 366/384). *Assistant Clerk* 1 April–31 May 1859 (ibid.). Left office 31 May 1859 on app. as Secretary to Lord High Commissioner, Ionian Islands (ibid.; *FOL* (Jan. 1860), 137).

Assistant Private Secretary to Secretary of State (Malmesbury) 26 Feb.–29 Oct. 1858 (FO 366/675 p. 9; *FOL* (Jan. 1859), 132).

Woodcock, Charles *Private Secretary to Secretary of State* (Harrowby) 5 July 1804–5 Jan. 1805 (FO 366/380). *Assistant Précis Writer* 5 Jan.–5 April 1805 (FO 366/1292, payment 15 Aug. 1805).

Woodford, John William Gordon *Assistant Junior Clerk* 12 Dec. 1845–14 Jan. 1849 (FO 366/674 p. 400; FO 366/383). *Junior Clerk* 14 Jan. 1849–1 July 1854 (FO 366/383–4). *Second Class Clerk* 1 July 1854–1 April 1857 (*FOL* (Aug. 1854), 9).

Assistant Clerk 1 April 1857–1 Dec. 1866 (*FOL* (July 1857), 9). *Senior Clerk* 1 Dec. 1866 (*FOL* (Jan. 1867), 7).

Woodgate, Arthur George Kennedy *Clerk* (*Chief Clerk's Dept.*) 23 Jan. 1867 (FO 366/676 p. 138).

Wrangham, Digby Cayley *Assistant Junior Clerk* 23 April 1827–25 April 1831 (FO 366/673 pp. 34–5; FO 366/381–2). Res. 25 April 1831 (FO 366/673 p. 163); elected M.P. 30 April 1831 (HC 69–I (1878) lxii, pt. ii, p. 333).

Private Secretary to Secretary of State (Dudley, Aberdeen) 30 April 1827–21 Nov. 1830 (FO 366/381–2).

Wylde, Everard William *Third Class Junior Clerk* 25 May 1868 (FO 366/676 p. 273; FO 366/257–8).

Wylde, William Henry *Extra Clerk* 14 March 1838–5 April 1839 (FO 366/673 pp. 349, 364). *Assistant Junior Clerk* 5 April 1839–16 Aug. 1841 (FO 366/382). *Junior Clerk* 16 Aug. 1841–12 Dec. 1845 (FO 366/394, 16 Aug. 1841; FO 366/382–3). *Second Class Clerk* 12 Dec. 1845–1 Jan. 1855 (FO 366/383–4). *Probationary Senior Clerk* 1 Jan. 1855–1 Jan. 1856 (FO 366/449 pp. 367–9; FO 366/384). *Second Class Clerk* 1 Jan. 1856–1 April 1857 (FO 366/449 p. 413; FO 366/384). *Assistant Clerk* 1 April 1857–1 Jan. 1859 (*FOL* (July 1857), 9). *Senior Clerk* 1 Jan. 1859 (*FOL* (Jan. 1859), 9).

Superintendent of Commercial and Consular Dept. 3 July 1869 (FO 366/676 pp. 464–5).

Wynn, Thomas Edward *Clerk* 21 April 1796–17 Feb. 1802 (FO 366/670 p. 391). Res. 17 Feb. 1802 (FO 366/671 p. 203).

Wynn *see also* **Williams Wynn**

Index of Offices